Beginners' Guide to Antique Watches

Carl & Maria-Luise Sifakis

DRAKE PUBLISHERS INC. NEW YORK•LONDON

To Ivan, who makes the watches run on time

*All photographs courtesy of Sotheby Parke Bernet, Inc.
Copyright Sotheby Parke Bernet, Inc., New York.*

Published in 1978 by
Drake Publishers, Inc.
801 Second Ave.
New York, N.Y. 10017

Copyright © 1978 by Carl Sifakis
All rights reserved

Library of Congress Cataloging in Publication Data

Sifakis, Carl
  Beginner's guide to antique watches.

  Includes index.
  1. Clocks and watches—Collectors and collecting—
United States. I. Sifakis, Maria-Luise, joint author.
II. Title.
NK7484.S5   681'.114'075   77-15902
ISBN 0-8473-1654-8

Design: Harold Franklin

Printed in the United States of America

Contents

Chapter		
I	The Antique Watch Collector's Credo	/ 5
II	Early Watch History	/ 9
III	The Golden Age of Watches	/ 15
IV	Watches, Watches, Watches	/ 23
V	What Makes a Watch Tick	/ 32
	Collector's Gallery I	/ *33*
VI	America and Other Late Comers in Watches	/ 55
	Collector's Gallery II	/ *65*
VII	Tales of Famous Watches	/ 87
VIII	Should You Invest in Antique Watches	/ 94
	Collector's Gallery III	/ *97*

Appendix		
A	Important Dates in the History of Watches	/ 117
B	Prominent Watchmakers Around the World	/ 119
	Glossary	/ *124*
	Index	/ *126*

Chapter I

The Antique Watch Collector's Credo

Why collect watches? Why, indeed, collect any antiques? It is something inborn in man. He must collect things of beauty, and he must collect *old* things of beauty before they disappear, never to be seen and enjoyed again. Man does it individually and collectively. After all, what are museums but expressions of man's inevitable urge to collect the real treasures of our cultural and historic past.

But why collect watches? To a true *afficionado* it is the thing to collect. An antique watch is something that "lived" in our historic past. It is history, but it still lives.

Queen Elizabeth I was one of the first to have the idea of wearing a small watch on a band around the wrist. That watch, which still ticks today, is more of a link to Elizabeth than the jeweled crown she wore. It lived in the seventeenth century; it lives now.

Watches are the only "pets" that famous people left behind. Did the Empress Josephine fondle a dog more than she did her beloved wrist watch with a gold and pearl bracelet? Such a watch is a living link to a turbulent past. And does not a Tom Mix pocket watch recall our own days of innocence with its stern message on the metal back: "ALWAYS FIND TIME FOR A GOOD DEED . . . Tom Mix." The story of Lafayette's lost watch, narrated in full detail in another chapter, is an important part of our history.

The soldier's fascination with watches is undying. Does any veteran of World War II not remember that watches, far more than Lugers, were the G.I.'s favorite souvenir? Were the Russian soldiers who smashed into Berlin avenging the gutting of their homeland or liberating the enslaved peoples of Europe? Or were they collecting watches. The "liberating" of watches is not, after all, the worst crime of combat soldiers, and it is something understandable and predictable.

During the winter of 1861-62 "watch fever" swept the 3rd New Hampshire Infantry during the Civil War. There was not a man left unaffected, and soldiers walked around with watches in every pocket. Watch trading dominated the activity of the camp with men hovering around dying campfires into the small hours of the morning haggling over deals. In desperation, the top officers ordered the guards to clamp in irons any man who appeared to be acting like a watch fiend after taps. Eventually the watch fever broke, and the watches of the 3rd New Hampshire scattered throughout the Army. Someone who owns one of these watches today owns a very special piece of Civil War history.

Our history is richer in that the watch belonging to Captain G.H. Amidon, Company E, 4th Vermont Infantry, remains. The men of his company gave Captain Amidon the watch, appropriately engraved, as a token of their esteem and respect. Amidon was wounded at Cedar Creek and at the Wilderness, where 268 out of his regiment of 500 were killed or wounded. Today, every tick of the Amidon watch is a living memorial to that tragic loss during a tragic war. This, then, is the stuff—the romance—of antique watch collecting.

For the collector of antique watches, there is history for those who want history. For those who want beauty, there is exquisite design in gold, in diamonds, in enamel. For the technical minded, there are mechanisms from the simple to the most complicated, through which the development of watchmaking can be traced.

Come, get watch fever, become a watch fiend. But beware—antique watch collecting can be tricky. It can be expensive, too expensive, if you don't have all the knowledge you should have. But if you learn the rules, there is room for those of you on a big budget or on a very tiny one, and the hours of enjoyment you reap will make the cost seem even less important.

Antique watches are scarce, and many have rather stunning value. Most of the very valuable ones belong to museums or are in the private collections of the very wealthy. However, many other great antiques are still around. A foxy collector can find them in antique shops, at county fairs, at garage sales, or at flea markets.

The most basic thing to keep in mind is that none of these watches is a good timekeeper. When one does work, it will not work well and must be valued for its artistic or historic value. When you are buying an antique watch, judge its value by the design of the case and its condition. If the workmanship is poor or if it is ugly or broken in any way, the watch has comparatively little value. If a dealer proudly points out that the watch works, say simply, "Well, you mean that it ticks." Of course, you do want a watch that runs well, but beware of a sales pitch that says the watch keeps good time. Really old antiques are marvelous if they lose only two hours a day. If the watch you are judging keeps good time, it is not a genuine antique, or it is one that has been so doctored that you should wonder how much of it is the real thing.

It is not always easy to pinpoint the age of an antique watch. Sometimes the watch is dated, but the question then arises as to when the date was put on. We have seen watches made by a certain watchmaker that were dated fifty to one hundred years before the watchmaker was born.

This book contains a fairly long list of important American and European watchmakers. It should be consulted when you try to determine the age of a watch. If the watch carries the name of the maker, its approximate age can be determined.

Some English watches have cases that carry a hallmark. This symbol will give the age. Other watches have no name, no hallmark, and no date. In such cases, its age must be figured out by studying the movement and the case. Cases vary in size, shape, type and method of decoration, form of pendant, and the way in which the movement is fastened to the case. Movements, depending on when they were made, vary in the pillars, hands, balance cock, fusee, dial, escapement, and screws.

By a little detective work, then, you can answer the question of age. Incidentally, this detective work should also be done where the date or watchmaker's name appears. Caution is always the password, not because there is a crooked world out there but because this is part of the joy of watch collecting. A watch is a watch not *because* it ticks, but rather *how* it ticks and *why* it ticks. There is pleasure in spotting the spurious, as well as in identifying the real.

Unfortunately, many antique watches have been renovated, rebuilt and, sometimes, almost totally changed. At times, parts of several other watches have been added. Later, other improvements are made. The artistic value of the original watch is, of course, lost. All too often, changes are made to improve an old watch so that it may be foisted on an unwary collector.

No hard and fast rule can be set on the current price of antique watches, except, of course, all are up and up considerably. On any particular watch, several factors must be considered: age, the condition of the watch, the importance and fame of the maker, the amount of jewels used in the case, and so on. A particular clockwatch of the mid-sixteenth century with an iron movement might be worth $1000 to $1500. Others of the same period might vary in price from $250 to $10,000. Attend any auction or private sale that you can, not simply to buy, but to add to your knowledge of values.

Successful antique watch collecting is often hard work, but it is always a labor of love.

Chapter II
Early Watch History

Watches are not nearly as old as most laymen tend to believe. They date back to the beginning of the sixteenth century. Even so, the origin of the watch is steeped in the fog of history. Who invented the watch? Well, who invented baseball? If you accept the legend that the father of baseball was Abner Doubleday, then by the same suspension of doubt, you can accept Peter Henlein as the father of the watch.

The invention of the mainspring is usually attributed to a young German locksmith, Peter Henlein of Nuremberg, about 1500. He is said to have used a long, tightly coiled ribbon of steel as the driving power in a timepiece instead of the weights that had been used in clocks up till that time.

Actually there are many references to small clocks that can be moved about. Undoubtedly some of these were actually watches. At the start of the sixteenth century there seemed to be great interest in a timepiece that could be worn on the belt, or on a bunch of keys, or hung from a cord around the neck.

Certainly Peter Henlein, or Heinlein, Henle, or Hele, as he is often referred to in various written records, was among the first watchmakers. In *Cosmographia Pomponii Melae* published in Nuremberg in 1511, it says, "Every day finer things are being invented. Peter Hele, still a young man, has constructed a piece of work which excited the admiration of the most learned mathematicians. He shapes many-wheeled watches out of small bits of iron, which run without weights for forty hours, however they may be carried, in pocket or chemisette.

There is no doubt that the last part of the fifteenth century and the first fifty years of the next was one of the most exciting epochs in the history of clockmaking. Weight-driven clocks were not portable; they were for home or public or business. Springdriven timepieces were new curiosities, and they were portable. Their appeal to the very rich was instantaneous.

Henlein's watches had iron movements mounted in

musk balls. The musk ball was a perforated metal sphere, often decorated, into which musk was put. It was worn much as scent is worn today. Other musk ball-type watches turned up elsewhere in Germany and in Blois, France.

The first watches, or perhaps we should call them clock-watches, were purse-sized versions of drum-shaped table clocks. Perhaps they should be considered the real "father" of the watch since by their shape they were the truer progenitors of the watch.

These clock watches were several inches in diameter. Their dials were of brass, chased or engraved, very heavily gilt, and there was only one hand. There was usually an outer ring of hour numerals from I to XII and an inner ring in Arabic numbers from 13 to 24. This suited the 24 system of timekeeping then in style. In German watches the covers of these had pairs of holes so that the numerals could be seen. A good way to pinpoint a sixteenth century German watch is by the 2 in the Arabic numbers. It is engraved like a Z.

Note the difference between chase and engraved work. In engraving the material has been cut away to form the pattern. In chasing the pattern has been made by pounding, rubbing, or pressing either from the front or underside.

The watches and case were most often hinged together, but many watches had pressed or snapped-on features.

As has already been mentioned, the works were of steel or iron. The parts of the movement were kept together by pins and wedges. Screws were not used. The mainspring, of course, was the driving mechanism, and the controlling mechanism was the crown wheel, the verge, and the foliot balance. This type of controlling mechanism remained in use in all timekeepers until 1658. As time went by, brass wheels made an occasional appearance, and not long after 1550, plates and screws came into use.

Through an error by a translator, all these early watches have been called "Nuremberg eggs." The translator mistook *Uerulein* (little clocks) for *Eierlein* (little eggs), and the mistake has stuck ever since.

While Nuremberg in Germany and Blois in France were two of the early watchmaking capitals, they were not the only ones. The Italians were into watches quite early, but documentation is lacking. The French industry really outdistanced the German as watchmaking quickly spread to

Paris, Rouen, Sedan, Lyon, Dijon, Grenoble, and elsewhere. Technically, too, they were the best, and their domination became almost total in the first part of the seventeenth century when the Thirty Years' War drained German economic strength. The English got into the game much later although there are records of some good early watchmakers at work in London.

What makes it difficult to ascribe certain characters to various countries is the international flavor to watchmaking. Apprentices often trained in other countries, Paris and Geneva being important teaching areas. After a young man completed his apprenticeship, he became a journeyman and would either return to his hometown or join other watchmakers in other important centers. Some became specialists in a certain aspect of the work, making watch mechanisms, or their various parts in series for sale to other watchmakers. This in-the-trade service went on between different workshops, even different cities and, in fact, different countries. An Italian or English watch might have many parts from Switzerland and an equal number, perhaps, from Germany or France.

The craft organization of labor governed the development of the watchmaking trade. Since gold came to be used in watches, a division of the work on a watch had to be done by a goldsmith. By the 1650s, there were at least six different crafts engaged in the production of watches: watchmaker, jeweller, engraver, goldsmith, enameller, and lapidary casemaker.

However, an equally important reason for the international flavor in watchmaking was the matter of religion and the ensuing intolerance. Blois was a stronghold of Huguenot or French protestant thought, and with the revocation of the Edict of Nantes in 1685, many Huguenot watchmakers began leaving the country, mainly for England and Switzerland, where their beliefs did not invite persecution. All this tended to internationalize the watch even more. Differences in watches among the various countries tended to disappear. A Geneva or London watch might bear the name of a French watchmaker, for example. The name of the city on the watch often is the only sure way to tell where many watches were finished.

One thing, however, remained constant about early

watches. They were terrible timekeepers. The villain in the piece was the very object that made the watch possible—the mainspring. When it was wound up, it pulled hard, but when it was well run down, the pull was much less. Naturally this greatly influenced the running time.

The Germans made the first big corrective step to the problem with the development of the stackfreed. The origin of the word is not known, and there is some speculation that it is from the Persian, but the connection is lost. The stackfreed consisted of a strong curved spring and cam. The spring was open, and the outend was attached to one of the movement's pillars. There was a small pinion fitting over the winding square that drove the wheel which was pivoted on the back plate. By leaving a few teeth on this wheel uncut, restriction was put on the spring to prevent its running down totally or from being too wound. The wheel also bore a cam which received pressure from a tiny roller, itself attached to the end of a second spring, whose other end was mounted on the back plate. In short, what happened was that when the mainspring was wound up and pulled with its top force, the stackfreed spring was raised, and thus the power of the mainspring was lessened. Then, when the mainspring was almost run down and its power lessening, the end of the stackfreed spring fell into the curved depression in the cam and was able to lend a small amount of added power. To a certain extent, the uneven pull of the mainspring could be equalized.

The other attempt at regulating the pull of the mainspring was the fusee. Studying the drawings of Leonardo da Vinci, Jacob Zech of Prague pioneered the development of the fusee. It consists of a coneshaped pulley upon which a catgut cord is wound. The other end of the cord is wound around the barrel containing the mainspring. With one end of the mainspring fastened to a fixed central arbor, the other end is fastened to the inside of the barrel. The barrel, meanwhile, rides free on its arbor. When the mainspring is wound up, it can easily pull the cord from the smallest groove of the conical pulley. But as the mainspring continues to unwind, more leverage is needed to uncoil the chain from the grooves of the increasingly larger diameter. By shaping the fusee to fit the mainspring's pull, an overall uniform pull is achieved. The fusee, in effect, provides a variable gear ratio and was a stroke of brilliance, fully worthy of the genius of Leonardo.

Which was superior, the stackfreed or the fusee? It was no contest. The fusee was the best. One noted authority of the last century mused that it was hard to understand the simultaneous existence of two devices for the same purpose when one was so clearly superior. The only pluses for the stackfreed over the fusee was that watches equipped with the former ran for a longer period between windings, and the latter required a rather large depth between plates and added an extra wheel to the train. Overall, the fusee seems to be far more popular at most watchmaking centers, outside of Germany. Within Germany, the stackfreed prevailed. One might ascribe it all to German stubborness.

While, for their time, both the stackfreed and fusee were remarkable achievements that made possible the popularization of the watch, their technical accomplishments can be overstated. Watches remained horrible timekeepers. One of the greatest improvements in accuracy was achieved through the invention of the balance spring in 1674, but even then, watches could not have been very accurate.

All these conclusions have to be drawn from suppositions since there is no written record in books, newspapers, or even diaries that tell us how well watches ran. There is no doubt, however, that the average watch owner was forever adjusting his watch whenever he spied a clock of unquestioned better accuracy.

It is clear from the way in which watches were used at the beginning of the eighteenth century that they were not very reliable. In *Souvenirs of Duguay-Trouin*, it is related that in 1703, five important war vessels were sent to prey on Dutch fishing vessels off the shores of Spitzenburg. During the summer, in latitude 81° where the sun would have been visible all day long, the craft were caught in a very dense fog, and for nine days there was no sun to help form any notion of the time of day. On the lead ship, time was kept with thirty-minute sandglasses. When the fog finally lifted and the sun appeared, allowing the time to be gauged, it was discovered that the sandglasses has made an error of eleven hours. The important thing to consider was that at the beginning of the eighteenth century, there was not a single watch on this important naval operation. Preference was given to the sandglass, which produced an error of about an hour a day. From this we conclude that watches of the day were performing *worse* than an error of one hour a day.

None of this knocks the value of the first watches. The real value of these early antiques depends on the facts that they were first, and they are rare. A stackfreed may be inferior to a fusee, but if in your watch-hunting you come across a stackfreed, you have a real winner. Perhaps a rotten timekeeper, but a marvelous antique!

Chapter III

The Golden Age of Watches

With some of the technical problems of watches alleviated, if not truly solved, by the stackfreed and then the fusee, interest in watches, by both their makers and their buyers, turned to the important matter of beauty. There was a great desire to get away from the cylindrical box—that is, the drum shape. By late in the sixteenth century, the French had turned to oval-shaped watches. Actually the sides were still like the drum watch, but the back and cover became slightly dome shaped.

Then the sides of watches were given a convex shape so that the oval watch with curved sides became the mode of the early 1600s. Of course, what this rounding effect did was lead to the pocket watch. Of course, these watches were still too big and, in fact, were never carried in the pocket, but the inevitable inventive trend was set.

At the same time, even before 1600, watches started to take on wild but artistic form. There were watches in the form of books, stars, fruit, animals, flowers, padlocks, crosses, insects, and cockleshells. The so-called "death's head" watch, simulating a skull, came into existence at this time. Brass had been used in most watches but now gold, silver, and rock crystal took over. Cases were often decorated with precious stones. It became the custom to carry the watches suspended from a chain around the neck or fastened to one's clothing.

In this golden age of watches, Blois became the case-making capital of the world. It is suspected that many, perhaps most, of the supposedly English cases of the early and mid-1600s were made in Blois. One is hard put to distinguish between a French and English case of the period.

Of course, similarity of decoration grew out of the prevalent practice of using pattern books. What Hogarth did for jewellers and Sheraton, Adam, and Chippendale for furniture makers, pattern book artists did for watch case makers. The best of these was, possibly, Antoine Jacquard of Poitiers, who leaned heavily to human figures, many in erotic positions.

Some English watches did, however, have one distinctive feature, an engraved border around the dial and the back plate. Around the 1650s, as circular cases began replacing oval cases, the engravings of human figures on the cases shifted to tulips and fritillary, a sort of lily.

About 1610 we see the appearance, for the first time, of watch glasses. Glasses were used in table clocks and clock-watches somewhat earlier than for watches. At first the glasses were on the thick side and quite flat. Split bezel rings were used to hold them in place. With the passage of time, watchmakers began experimenting with watch glasses that were more rounded and higher.

As has been noted, the shape of cases was undergoing steady change. The greatest change of all was brought about by the colorful use of enamels and enamel painting. Enamelling was a very old decorative art that started in the East. Long before the invention of the watch, new processes for enamelling were found, and the art found a new home in Europe. The trade flourished in Switzerland, Holland, Germany (in Mosam), and of course in Limoges, France.

Enamel is actually glass, being composed of potash, red lead, and silica, which is melted onto a metal surface, such as gold or copper, and sometimes brass for watch cases, and bronze and iron for other purposes. By altering the proportions of its contents, the melting temperature of the enamel can be varied. With a low temperature a "soft" enamel results. In soft enamelling, long exposure to the atmosphere will often cause deterioration. In high temperature or "hard" enamel the original color and surfacing will last indefinitely, but the price that is paid is its quick tendency to crack, both from sudden shocks or from temperature variations between the enamel and its metal backing.

The first forms of decorative enamelling for watches show up on German watches before 1600. It was called champlevé enamelling and appeared first on the dial and then on the case as well. The process called for the pattern to be made by carving or hollowing the surface with a graver, resulting in walls of metal up to the original level of the surface. Each compartment is filled with the appropriate color, gradations of which can be obtained by varying the depth of the cells. The metal is then fired in a furnace until the frit of color melts and turns into colored glass in each compartment.

In a variation of this method, the surface of the metal was formed into a pattern of cells by fixing thin strips of metal, usually gold, onto a plate, with the strip edges being the outlines of the design. The strips themselves were either fixed to the plate or kept in place by a thin layer of enamel on the plate. This form of enamelling was called "cloisonné." Cloisonné was used only on watch dials while champlevé was adaptable for use on both cases and dials. It is more or less agreed that the most beautiful example of cloisonné enamel is on a watch done by Jacques Huon of Paris. Huon put each flower in a cell formed by a cloison that is so fine that it is barely visible. The stems and pistils are the top edges of the cloison, in this case, deliberately made thick enough to be visible. Huon shaded the individual flowers by the process of painting on enamel. Dating from approximately 1650, the watch is in the Victoria and Albert Museum in London. Regrettably this watch and another one in Dresden, are the only ones by Houn that are now known to exist.

Painting in enamel at Limoges started at the same time as the first appearance of the watch, about 1500, and flourished for a century and then went into decline. However, this method was not highly suitable for watches, and not too many of such examples exist today. About 1630 a revolutionary method of painting on enamel was discovered by a French goldsmith, Jean Toutin. Toutin's method called for painting oxides onto a ground of white enamel, with the most delicate results. This was the method the watch was crying for. Regrettably, no work done by Toutin has now been identified, but watches by his sons, Jean and Henri, do exist.

Painted enamel watches became the pride of Blois. A whole roster of Blois masters who painted on enamel developed, and today their works are among the most sought after antiques. Some of the names on any collector's "Most Wanted List" would include:

- Isaac Gribelin, master before 1634

- Dubie, believed to have been one of Toutin's first pupils
- Pierre Chartier, a master at the age of twenty in 1638, a specialist in flowers
- Christophe Morliere, another great painter in flowers
- Jacques Poete, flowers
- Blaise Floucher, the renowned painter of the legends of Theseus and Antiope and Hippolyta

Other painters on enamel are worthy of mention. There is the work of Nicolas Bernard of Paris and Goullens of Paris. Robert Vauquer, son of the engraver and watchmaker Michel Vauquer, carried on Morliere's vogue and even outclassed him in skill.

In the second half of the sixteenth century, a family of painters became dominant. They were the Huaud family of Geneva. The first, Pierre Huaud, was a goldsmith who painted on enamel. He was outdone by the works of all three of his sons, Jean, Pierre, and Ami. Of the three, Pierre was the best painter. He went to the Court of Brandenburg, and in 1691 he was appointed painter to the Elector. Pierre signed his work in various ways, such as: Pierre Huaud, Petrus Huaud major natus, Huaut l'aisné, P. Huaud primogenitus.

Jean's work can be found under the name of Huaud le puisné. Jean often worked with his brother Ami, and the pair were appointed painters to the Court of Prussia in 1686. They returned to Geneva in 1700. Samples of their work, prize possessions of museums and collectors, are signed variously: Les deux frères Huaut les jeunes, Les frères Huard, Peter et Amicus Huaut, or Fratres Huault.

In technique the work of the Huaud family was brilliant, but some criticism could be made that their colors were hard and tended to be garish. Perhaps they won as much fame for the subjects of their pictures, which were often of very buxom ladies only partly clothed.

The Huaud family was primarily responsible for making Geneva famous for enamelling, and for the gradual shift there from Blois, for political and religious reasons, as well as artistic ones. Today one would have to regard Geneva as the enamelling capital of the world. Most of the advances in enamelling were made there. One of the earliest new methods of enamelling was "basse-taille" in which a very thin layer of translucent enamel was laid over an engraved plate. In the latter half of the seventeenth century, perhaps around 1670 at the earliest, "flinqué" became the rage. This was the employment of enamelling over a regular pattern of hand engraving.

By the end of the eighteenth century, Geneva had expanded enamelling as a craft to the state that Swiss enamelled watches, musical boxes, and many other novelties were being shipped all over the world.

Enamelling did much to give impetus to the desire to have a pocket watch. They were now works of art worthy of being carried. Then in the last quarter of the seventeenth century, two developments, one in technology and one in fashion, profoundly influenced the development of the watch. The balance spring was the technological advance.

Just after 1600, there were some watches that used a straight hog's bristle to curb the motions of the balance. In 1658 the Englishman Robert Hooke started trying to use a straight metal spring instead of the hog's bristle. In 1674, working quite independently of one another, Abbe Hautefeuille of France and Christian Huygens of Holland each used a spirally coiled metal spring. It is now impossible to tell who invented the balance spring; suffice it to say that the work of Hautefeuille, Huygens, and Hooke were all instrumental, and by 1675 we had the balance spring.

The second development, this one in the world of fashion, was equally as important in the development of the pocket watch. It was the introduction of the waistcoat. Suddenly, there was a convenient place for a gentleman to carry a watch. While most early pocket watches were enamelled, this would, in time, become less important. It was the Puritan style to conceal the watch, and the need for decoration, therefore, started to decrease. Eventually, this trend toward less decoration heralded the epoch of the lower priced watch.

But whether a watch was artistically enamelled or was a plain case of brass, silver, or gold, it was customary to have an outer protective case to keep the valuable watch from being scratched or smudged. This custom of having two cases for a watch was called "pair cases."

The outer case could be made of brass or wood or shagreen, among other materials. These soft materials were usually placed on a metal foundation. Brass and shagreen were the most used. Shagreen could be either sharkskin or horsehide, finished in a distinctive way and colored green. As a leading authority, Britten, puts it: "The true shagreen is a remarkably tough kind of leather, made chiefly at Astrachan from the strong skin that covers the crupper of the ass or horse. In its preparation a peculiar roughness is produced by treading into the skin hard round seeds, which are shaken out when the skin has been dried; it is then stained green with copper filings and salammoniac, and the grains or warts are then rubbed down to a level with the rest of the surface, which thus presents the appearance of white dots on a green ground. The skin of the shark and of various other fishes, when properly prepared, formed an excellent covering, being thin and durable. This if dyed green was also known as shagreen."

The protective case when made of shagreen, or for that matter tortoiseshell or fish skin, was studded usually with gold or silver nails in some sort of geometric pattern. When brass was used, it was usually chased with the figures standing out in bold relief. This technique was called "repoussé" chasing.

Decorations of watches were not limited to the case and the dial. Movements were lavishly decorated or engraved on the back plate. Two parts of a watch movement that were very much ornamented were the watch pillars and the balance cocks.

The watch pillar was the posts that held the two plates of a watch movement together. Nowadays watch pillars are very simple pieces of brass and are visible only when the movement is taken out of its case. In the early days of watches, the pillars were visible when a hinged movement had to be lifted up to be wound. That was reason enough to lavish decoration on them. The pillars are an excellent way for a collector to date an antique watch. The first pillars were of a rather simple baluster style, but by the mid-1600s, watchmakers came up with a variety of new shapes, most popular of which was probably the tulip pillar. By about 1700, an Egyptian pillar came into vogue. It was a tapered affair and does not appear to be much in use before the end of the sixteenth century, making watches so equipped easy to date. There were also plainer square pillars, but they were popular at all times during this period and thus make a poor historical marker.

The balance cock was the projecting bar that held one of the bearings of the balance. The balance cocks were quite large and the subject of heavy decoration. They could be carved and pierced. They were sometimes made of brass and sometimes had an enamel painting fitted on them. Balance cocks changed regularly in design, starting first as an ordinary "S" shape to a pierced oval with a pierced foot. The foot was often patterned into foliage decoration. By the mid-1600s, the cocks were round in shape and had become much bigger. As the century progressed, the cocks grew smaller, and the foot of the balance had become wedge shaped, with the curved outer edge following the circular edge of the movement. Circular balance cocks were patterned symmetrically until almost 1750 when the styles changed to asymmetrical patterns. Still later, balance cocks became both narrower and tapered.

The early attempts to achieve a plain watch did not prevent the decoration of the balance cock. Even before 1650, the Puritan watch made its appearance in England. These watches were quite small, egg shaped, and sported a plain silver case with no ornamentation or simple engraving. The dials, too, were plain silver and had only a steel hand covered by a glass. Yet even in these Puritan watches, the movement remained equipped with the elaborated pierced balance cock. Plain was fine, but there was no need to be pigheaded about it.

Now, in this golden age of watches, one type of watch after another came spewing out at the consumer, some good, some better, and some terrible. Even in its youthful prime, the watch industry could have had a Better Business Bureau to rein it in.

A case in point is the so-called pendulum watch. These were the products of more or less second-rank watchmakers, capitalizing on the average person's ignorance about the principles of watchmaking. One thing the public did know was that clocks of that era were far more accurate than watches, and that this accuracy was due largely to the pendulum on clocks. Well, if you could have a pendulum clock, why not a pendulum watch?

That made perfect sense, save for one minor detail. A

pendulum will not work on a watch. This, however, did not deter some makers. People wanted a pendulum watch, so they gave them a pendulum watch. All that was necessary was to rearrange the watch movement so that the balance wheel was located right under the dial instead of its old place over the top plate on the other side of the watch.

The dial was designed with a curved slot in it, and a tiny disc, resting on the balance rim, could be seen swinging in the slot. Naturally, the watchmakers counted on the public's being impressed with this meaningless blob. Since it was swinging back and forth like a pendulum bob, this blob seemed to indicate that the watch had the virtues of a pendulum clock. Actually this bit of fakery had at least one value to the gullible buyer. He had merely to glance at his watch to tell if it had stopped.

The misvalue of the pendulum watch, aside from the fact that it was a confidence swindle, was the added demerit that the balance was moved from a position of easy accessibility, which was important. Some Dutch and French makers attacked this problem and came up with a mechanism that returned the balance to its correct position. Fine workmanship, after a fashion, had been restored. The pendulum gimmick was no longer hurting the watch, and, happily, this misrepresentation to the public could continue.

Chapter IV

Watches, Watches, Watches

Late in the sixteenth century, repeater watches were invented. The owner of a repeater watch could have his watch struck on either one or two gongs, no matter when the watch was set to repeat. There were six-hour repeaters, hour repeaters, quarter repeaters, half-quarter repeaters, five-minute repeaters, and even minute repeaters. The mechanism became more complex as the time interval narrowed.

Exactly who invented the repeater watch is another matter in dispute. It was either Edward Barlow or Daniel Quare, both of England. Barlow had invented the rack striking works for clocks, which led to the repeating mechanism about 1676. Ten years later, Barlow made a repeating watch based on the same tenets and applied for a patent. But Daniel Quare had also adapted the clock mechanism to watches, and he opposed Barlow's claim. Eventually the king, James II, made a decision in the matter after trying both watches. He ruled in favor of Quare, because his was simpler to operate. However this was not the way to decide which man had invented the repeater.

Most laymen would probably be surprised to hear that stem-wound and stem-set watches are only a little more than a century old. Up until that time, a watch owner was obliged to open the case of a watch each time he wished to set or wind it. This meant not only carrying the watch around, but a watch key as well. Some museums sport full collections of watch keys because many of them were themselves things of beauty on which the watchmaker lavished much attention. Many watch owners appreciated the fact that a key was needed to wind the watch because if the watch was pinched by a pickpocket, it was of less value to him without a key. Of course, he could go to a maker for a duplicate, but this certainly increased the chance of detection. Rather than risk it, some criminals cannibalized stolen watches, selling the valuable and melting down the gold. Many priceless watches, by today's standards, were lost to posterity by such acts.

Within two hundred years of the first watch—around 1700 or perhaps a bit earlier—the first keyless watches turned up. Generally, they were the work of some gifted individual who designed just one. It took a good century longer for various versions to be patented. These early keyless watches were not stem-winders as we have today. One version was wound by moving round a projection on the watch's side. Another version required that the stem be pushed in and out with a sort of pumping action. Among the important names to look for on keyless watches are Adrien Philippe who is credited with developing the shifting sleeve, keyless mechanism and Gustavus Hughenin, the holder of the patent on the rocking bar mechanism.

If the modern stem-winder took so long to develop, perhaps it is amazing that self-winding watches came along as early as they did, still in the 1700s. The earliest versions were called "pedometer watches" because a heavy pivoted weight, as in a pedometer, rocked to and fro with the movements of the wearer.

Some of the best self-winders or "perpetuelles," as they came to be known in France, were the work of Abraham-Louis Breguet who produced a great number of these before the French Revolution. Breguet is generally conceded to be the number one watchmaker (and clockmaker) of all time. When Richard Thomson set out to write a book about antique American clocks and watches, he quite naturally tried to limit the book to American makers and their English predecessors, but there was no way he could leave out this amazing Frenchman.

In Breguet's perpetuelles, a stop-work locked the weight when the spring was fully wound. And in order that the watch owner should know how far his watch was wound at any particular moment, his watches generally contained a subsidiary up-and-down dial.

Being a perfectionist, Breguet stopped making perpetuelles about 1800 unless he had a special order from a customer. Even his standards of workmanship, astronomical when compared with most others, were not enough to guarantee that the perpetuelles would operate with good regularity over the long haul.

More will be told later about this incredibly talented watchmaker. Suffice it to say here that the value of a perpetuelle or any of his other watches is very, very, very high. If his self-winders did not work to perfection, it was because the state of the art at the time had not advanced far enough. Breguet was defeated here by a watch that did not have a right to be born and, in reality, was not born until the 1930s.

Almost from the very beginning of the watch, makers thought they would show their skills by producing miniature watches. As early as 1542, the Duke of Urbino ordered a clock watch mounted in a ring. By about two centuries later, the state of the art of watchmaking had progressed so far that John Arnold could produce a small ring watch. It was a quarter repeater with one hundred twenty parts and yet was only one third of an inch across. Watches were also set in seals, balls, and miniature vases. The Empress Josephine had a wrist watch set into a gold and pearl bracelet.

It was the miniature watch idea that eventually led to the concept of the wrist watch. Queen Elizabeth I was one of the first women to sport a small watch on a band around the wrist. Still, the wrist watch was very slow in developing. As late as the mid-nineteenth century, the furthest the technique had gotten was that some Swiss makers had started to fit some of their miniature pocket watches into bracelets or attached them to velvet wristbands. The father of the wrist watch was probably E.A. Pearson, a saddler in London, who designed a watch to be held in a sort of leather cup, just before World War I. Later on he refined the technique by soldering wire lugs to which the halves of the strap were sewn onto the sides of the case.

Far more than thinking in terms of making a watch fit the wrist, early and mid-period watchmakers concentrated much more on developing attachments that would give the watch owner some specific service and enhance the maker's reputation. There were all sorts of attachments. They struck, chimed, alarmed, and repeated. There were chronographs, calendar, moon phases, and equation-of-time attachments. Some of these survive to the present day while others have simply disappeared.

We have already discussed repeaters but not the watches that struck the hours in the normal course, differing entirely from repeaters that struck when a projecting

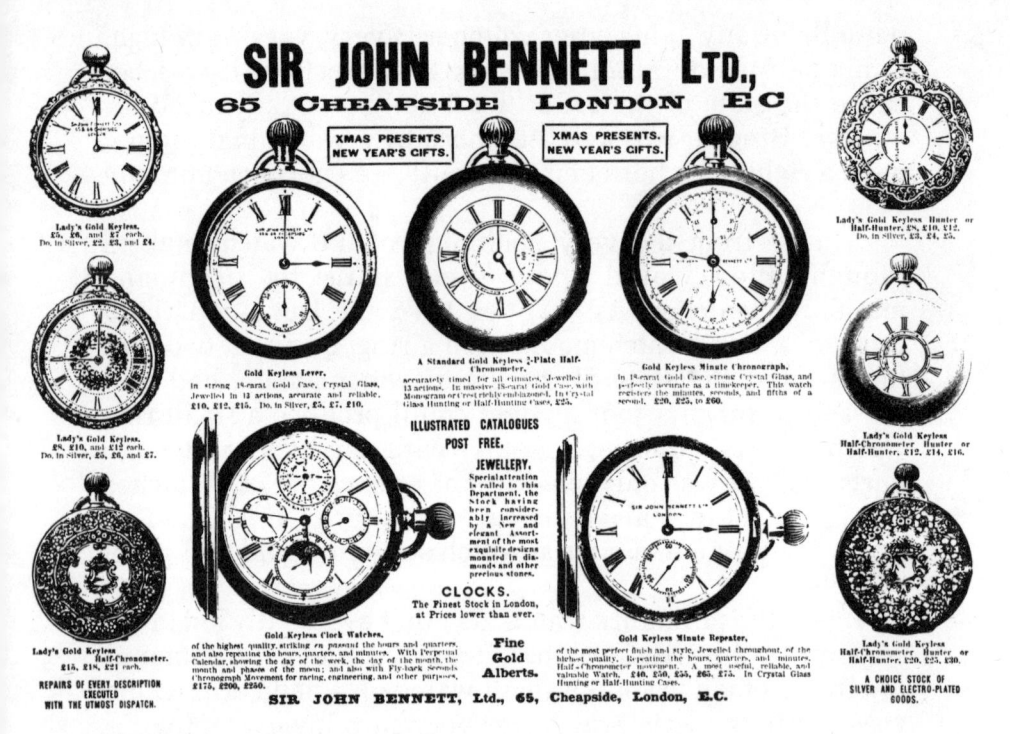

1895 ad from *Illustrated London News.*

slide was moved round or was pushed in. Some striking watches struck not only the hour but the quarter hour as well. Some were devised to strike before the hour to alert the wearer to some chore he had to perform on the hour. During the first one hundred years of the watch, the sixteenth century, well over half of all watches were striking watches of some sort. A striking watch was readily converted into a repeater since it was relatively simple to add an arrangement so that adjusting something outside would start the striking train inside. A problem that arose was if the striking watch was repeated too often, the striking part wore down much sooner than the time part.

Alarm attachments were also an early development. Such watches simply had practically the same mechanism as the alarm clock. While almost everyone—man, woman, and child—enjoyed a nice striking or chime, the fact was that striking watches steadily declined in popularity; at present there are almost none made. There were several reasons for this. In the first place, watch owners soon discovered that having a watch with a striking attachment made the cost of cleaning or repairing it so much more expensive than a watch without the device. Perhaps even more important was the fact that the attachments almost always caused the watch to keep poorer time, and the public was definitely opting, more and more, for accuracy in a timepiece. Then, too, the cost of making a simple alarm clock kept dropping so that the cost of making an alarm watch became less inviting because even when the watch struck, it did not make a really loud noise and could be easily heard only if the watch wearer stayed alert and listened for the sound.

But complications or no, there was great public appetite for unusual watches. There were watches with calendar and moon-phase attachments. There were others with equation-of-time attachments. These equation-of-time watches have all but disappeared in modern production. The world is now universally on standard time, and modern life is no longer connected with the rising and setting of the sun. Many watches in the pre-1600 era were equipped with an attachment that even gave the time the sun passed the meridian. Calendar watches were far more common than the attachment for the equation of time and existed in large numbers before 1600.

But as complicated watches went, these were child's play. Some watches had moving automatons which played out scenes. One watch, a part of the Morgan collection at the Metropolitan Museum of Art in New York, is from the eighteenth century and is either of German or Swiss origin. Faced in blue enamel with landscape, the watch has two mechanical figures grinding and hammering. The mechanism of the watch moves them. The dial, laid in the blue sky of the landscape, is surrounded with diamonds. All this is accomplished in a piece that is really quite thin and is only two inches in diameter.

A pair-case watch, also at the Metropolitan, a part of the Maurice M. Sternberger loan collection, is an astronomical type. Besides giving the time, it informs the watch wearer of the tides, the phases of the moon, the moon's age, the position of the sun, the sun's declination, and the month and day. The watch, by George Margetts, carries a London hallmark of 1783. Margetts watches are noted for their originality of design and their mechanical perfection.

However, when it comes to complicated watches, one produced by L. Leroy & Cie. may well have been the most complicated watch ever put together. It features, among other things: the days of the week, date of the month, dates for one hundred years, a perpetual calendar of the months, phases of the moon, seasons, solar time, chronograph, minute chronograph, hours chronograph, up-and-down winding hand, full striking and silence, three-gong minute repeater, Boreal sky—sidereal time and 460 stars, Austral sky—sidereal time and 250 stars, local time for 125 localities, sunrise, sunset, thermometer, hygrometer, barometer, mountain barometer, regulating system, and compass. It also tells the time! And all with just 975 parts!

Other types of complicated watches were musical ones which were introduced well before 1800. The Swiss and French were very adept at making these. Tunes could play either at specific times or at the discretion of the wearer. The musical attachment consisted of steel springs of specific length and thickness to produce certain notes. A rotating disc studded with pins would catch on or play the steel springs, producing music of surprisingly high quality. Naturally, these watches had to be thicker than most as room had to be allowed for the music disc as well as a separate spring to drive it. In addition, a great many musical watches had moving automatons as well. Not too many musical watches were made, their large size being against them.

The same knock can be given to the so-called "traveling watches." They had very big diameters, anywhere from three-to eight inches. They appeared almost with the first watches and remained in use until the advent of railroads. In the giant size, some were complicated watches with many attachments. Over a period of time, such traveling watches had to be one of the early casualities of man's hunt for a small, simple, and accurate watch.

In a sense, lever watches were a transition toward the simpler and cheaper watch. In the nineteenth century, many fine English watches appeared. These watches have never enjoyed the same collector appeal as Swiss watches because they were less ornamental, although many came in precious metal cases. The lever or "forked escapement" watch was invented by Thomas Mudge in 1770 but did not come into general use for another seventy or eighty years when it was revived by Josiah Emery and then Peter Litherland. The lever watch was a cheaper watch, but by 1850 it had become noted for quality work. The English lever pocket watch with fusee movement was exported in huge quantities and probably became the leading watch of its time. Its popularity ended only when the Swiss machine-made watches became dominant late in the nineteenth century.

Actually the Swiss were not the leaders in machine-made watches at first. The important producers were the French and then the Americans. Some of these early machine-made watches have become collector's items because of their ingenuity of construction and their rarity. One prize is the Waterbury watch. Invented by Daniel Buck, it was made by the Waterbury Watch Company during the last two decades of the nineteenth century. It had a mainspring that was almost nine feet long and was called the "old long wind Waterbury." It was a form of "tourbillon," an invention for neutralizing vertical position errors in a watch. However, the whole movement revolved in the case. It was the first watch with this technique to become a commercial success. The movement revolved once an hour around a fixed center wheel that was attached to the case. There was a simplified duplex escapement, and the watch was set by pushing the hands around. The entire watch was constructed out of only 58 parts, including all the screws and the case. Unlike the English and Swiss watches of the period, all parts of the Waterbury were hand stamped from sheet metal rather than being hand finished.

Another American watch that falls into the collector category was Ingersoll's "dollar watch," produced in the same period. The Swiss entry into the cheap race was the "Roscopf," produced by a man of the same name. Made in the 1860s, the movement was incredibly simple, in many respects very primitive in layout, but boasting, for the first time, new ideas such as the pin pallet escapement which remains in cheap wrist watches to the present day. To set the hands, it was necessary to open the hinged glass and push them around. The Belgian railways adopted the early Roscopfs for their employees, and they are the first examples of the "railroad watch."

There are a number of experts today who believe that the best speculation in antique watches remains in the form of the American railroad watch. The frontier scene of the switchman and conductor pulling out their trusty pocket watches is disappearing. Today's railroadmen are giving them up mainly because they simply cannot get the high caliber of watch they are required to have. The rules of the railroads call for an American-made watch with at least 21 jewels and accuracy within 30 seconds a week. The sad fact is that there really is no American pocket watch available that can meet those standards. Railroadmen are quietly switching to quartz-crystal, electronic wrist watches.

It is terribly unchic to use a wrist watch on a railroad. As far as keeping time, the electronic quartz watches achieve accuracy within 30 seconds a month, but there are no jewels at all. There are reports that some makers are considering production of an electronic pocket watch that would restore the proper decorum to the railroad scene. However, despite the dumping on the market of railroad watches, the collector demand still far outdistances the supply. Old pocket watches that were selling for $20 just a few years ago now command prices of $150. There are many who expect the escalation to continue.

No short chapter that seeks to discuss watches, simple or complicated, can do so without paying some attention to the works of Abraham-Louis Breguet. Without doubt, he dominated the watch scene during the half century of his active life, and he continued to dominate it long after his death. Breguet watches are worth a fortune, and for that reason, he has been very widely faked. The Breguet name on a watch is a signal for caution. It must be thoroughly checked out before it is accepted.

Breguet was born in Neuchatel, Switzerland, Jan. 10, 1747. He came to Paris early and set up a business. In 1787 he opened his own shop, and there, save for a break during the French Revolution, he sent forth a flood of watch masterpieces and technical advances unequaled by any other great master.

Unlike so many other great watchmakers, Breguet never published anything, so that he achieved his reputation solely through his inventions and the watches that survived him. He invented the "tourbillon" which was a revolving carriage in which the escapement was placed to avoid position errors. Says Britten: "It is practically impossible to adjust a watch so that it will maintain an unaltered rate in all positions. Breguet overcame this in some of his finest watches by mounting the balance and escape wheel on a movable platform geared to the third wheel, so that the platform makes a complete revolution, usually once a minute. Thus, all position errors recur and so, for practical purposes, cancel each other out. A tourbillon watch may have a lever or detent escapement, and some exceptional pocket watches are still made with it. It does, however, demand superlative standards of workmanship if the results are to be justified. The tourbillon was patented by Breguet in 1801, but a less exacting and equally effective variant was devised by Bonniksen of Coventry in 1894. He called it a 'karussel' in which the platform revolves only once in every 52½ minutes."

It is the measure of the man that his inventions and theories could stand for a century in a field in such technological flux. Breguet invented the "parachute." This was a sort of yielding, bearing surface for the balance staff pivots, to keep them from breaking. He also invented the overcoil hairspring; he developed his special form of ruby cylinder, the watch called "a tact," the self-winding watch, and designs in complex watches too numerous, perhaps too technical, to recount.

No wonder there are collectors who would consider it the epitome of their collections to have something so rare as pieces composed solely of Breguets!

Of course, other watch collectors specialize in other areas. The late King Farouk of Egypt had a big collection of pornographic watches. Switzerland, staid Switzerland, has always been one of the chief sources of pornographic watches, really churning them out in the latter part of the last century. At Sotheby's in England, they still recall, with some embarrassment, how the pornographic nature of one watch of Farouk's collection went undiscovered, slipped through, and was sold. Yes, it really was sold to a clergyman and, yes, he was showing it to a lady and, yes, he accidentally pushed the secret spring and, yes...

Chapter V

What Makes a Watch Tick

It is no simple task to tell how a watch works, certainly not if one attempts to trace all the developments that took place in the last five hundred years. In this chapter, we will discuss the matter broadly since a novice will learn it best over the years as he gets into collecting.

The driving power of the watch or "power unit," is supplied by the mainspring. This was most likely invented by Peter Henlein. In the modern watch, most movements have the same number of wheels, springs, and other parts. They are laid out in a regular pattern with each part found in the same place. This can't be said of old watches. For instance, Henlein made improvements in almost each watch he made, always experimenting, always producing something new.

What the watch did, that clocks before it did not do, was contain its own power. Clocks until then used weights that acted with gravitational pull to provide power. This was what limited the clock to a fixed position on a shelf, or wall, or even on the tower of some mighty building. Henlein came up with a strip of iron or steel ribbon that he wound around an axle fastened to the largest gear in the clock. At first, Henlein created a small clock with built-in power. The force that was created by the unwinding of this springy metal ribbon rotated the wheels.

Mainsprings, being of different length, width, and thickness, vary according to the size of the watch. There has to be a ratchet and click to keep the mainspring from uncoiling as soon as it is wound. First we have the mainspring, and we attach it at its inner end to a hook on a small spool called the "barrel arbor." The barrel arbor is the axle of the barrel, which is a flat, round, hollow container with gear teeth around its outer circumference. The mainspring, attached to the barrel arbor, is wound around the arbor and set into the barrel. The outer end of the mainspring is hooked to a connection or brace onto the inside of the barrel. Then, as the mainspring forces the barrel around, the gear teeth around the barrel's edge will propel any gear or pinion contacting them.

Collector's Gallery I

**Rare Silver-Gilt Bird-Form Watch —
Choudens et Chauannes, Paris —
Circa 1650**

The oval-shaped verge movement has cock in the form of a floral spray, ratchet set-up, and regulator. Silver dial has single blued steel hand and is bordered with engraved ferns. The body of the bird is chased with feathers. The crested head has ruby eyes. Feet are webbed. Peacock tail was most probably added later. Authors' Fair Price Estimate: $6,000 *(top)* **Silver Pair Case Verge Watch with Calendar** — Joseph Windmills, London — Late 17th century

Large verge movement with fine tulip pillars surmounted with scrolls. The cock is pierced with a stylized spray of foliage with a matching spreading foot. The back plate is engraved in another hand AD 1676. The silver dial has an outer calendar ring and black enamel numerals and is centered by the maker's name in a baroque cartouche. One hand is missing. The outer case is covered with tortoiseshell and engraved with a girl beside a windmill (in reference to the maker), within a pique point border. The bezel is decorated with tortoiseshell. Authors' Fair Price Estimate: $1,000.

(bottom) **Attractive German Gilt-Metal and Enamel Openface Watch** — I.S. Egger, Berlin — Circa 1760

The verge movement has quadrangular baluster pillars. The bridge is pierced with foliage and a monster head. White enamel dial has blued steel beetle and poker hands. The back is enamelled with a seated couple in a landscape. Sprays of flowers are enamelled on the bezel. The inside is decorated with a bouquet of flowers painted in enamel. Authors' Fair Price Estimate: $1,200.

Opposite page
(top, left) **Three-Color Gold and Enamel Lady's Openface Watch** — Signed L'Epine à Paris — Circa 1775

Verge movement with scroll-pierced cock. White enamel dial has one replaced hand. The back is enamelled with a miniature of a young woman wearing a rose at her bosom and a feather in her hair in a frame of silver-set pastes surmounted by a crown. The background is chased with varicolored floral sprays on a matted ground and has leaf-tip borders. Bezel is set with pastes. Authors' Fair Price Estimate: $900.

Collector's Gallery I

(top, right) **French Four-Color Gold Quarter Repeating Openface Watch** — Signed Musson à Paris, No. 215 — 1763

Has cylinder movement, later balance and regulator. White enamel dial has gold scrollwork hands. Repeating on the case and with button for pulse repeat. The case is finely chased with a garden trophy before a balustrade with a ruin on one side and a colonnade with fountain on the other. The background of sun-rays is bordered with scrolls of flowers. Authors' Fair Price Estimate: $1,200.

(bottom, right) **Dutch Silver Pair Case Calendar Watch** — Signed Jo. Wilter, London — Circa 1750

Verge movement has continental-style bridge pierced with scrolls and a monster head. Silver champlevé dial has arcaded chapter ring with gilt studs, pierced center with gilt plate below, calendar window, and gilt scrollwork hands. Repoussé outer case is chased with the Judgment of Solomon, signed Mauris fecit, within a cartouche bordered by urns of flowers. Authors' Fair Price Estimate: $850.

(top) **Four-Color Gold Openface Watch** — Signed Barthelo, Paris — Circa 1765

Verge movement. White enamel dial has gold scrollwork hands. The back is chased with basket of flowers on a sun-ray ground surrounded by scrollwork. Authors' Fair Price Estimate: $1,050.

(bottom) **Gold Thin Openface Quarter Repeating Watch** — Maker unknown — Circa 1810

In Breguet style. Cylinder movement has eight rubies, parachute, and compensation. Gold cuvette. Dial is engine-turned silver with gold hands. Case is also engine-turned. Authors' Fair Price Estimate: $650.

Opposite page
(left) **Fine English Gold, Enamel, and Diamond Openface Watch** — William Anthony, No. 1568, London — Circa 1790

Has elaborately chased gilt duplex movement. White enamel dial has gold hands and center seconds. The back is decorated with a patera of rose diamonds and pearls centered by a large rose diamond, all on a translucent blue enamel ground and bordered with gold trefoils within white enamel lines. The rims are set with a double border of large and small pearls. The pendant is also set with pearls. Authors' Fair Price Estimate: $7,000.

(top, right) **Gold Pair Case Watch** — John Shore, London — Circa 1735

Verge movement. White enamel dial has beetle and poker hands. The plain first case is hallmarked London 1735. Second case is repoussé and chased with classical figures surrounded by scrolls. Authors' Fair Price Estimate: $1,250.

(bottom, right) **Gold and Enamel Quarter Repeating Automaton Watch** — Maker unknown — Circa 1820

The small white dial of enamel is flanked by four-color gold figures of Orpheus and Eurydice striking bells with hammers. A figure of Cupid strikes a third bell at the base. All are on a blue enamel ground. The case is engine-turned and is signed Breguet et fils. Authors' Fair Price Estimate: $2,100.

Collector's Gallery I

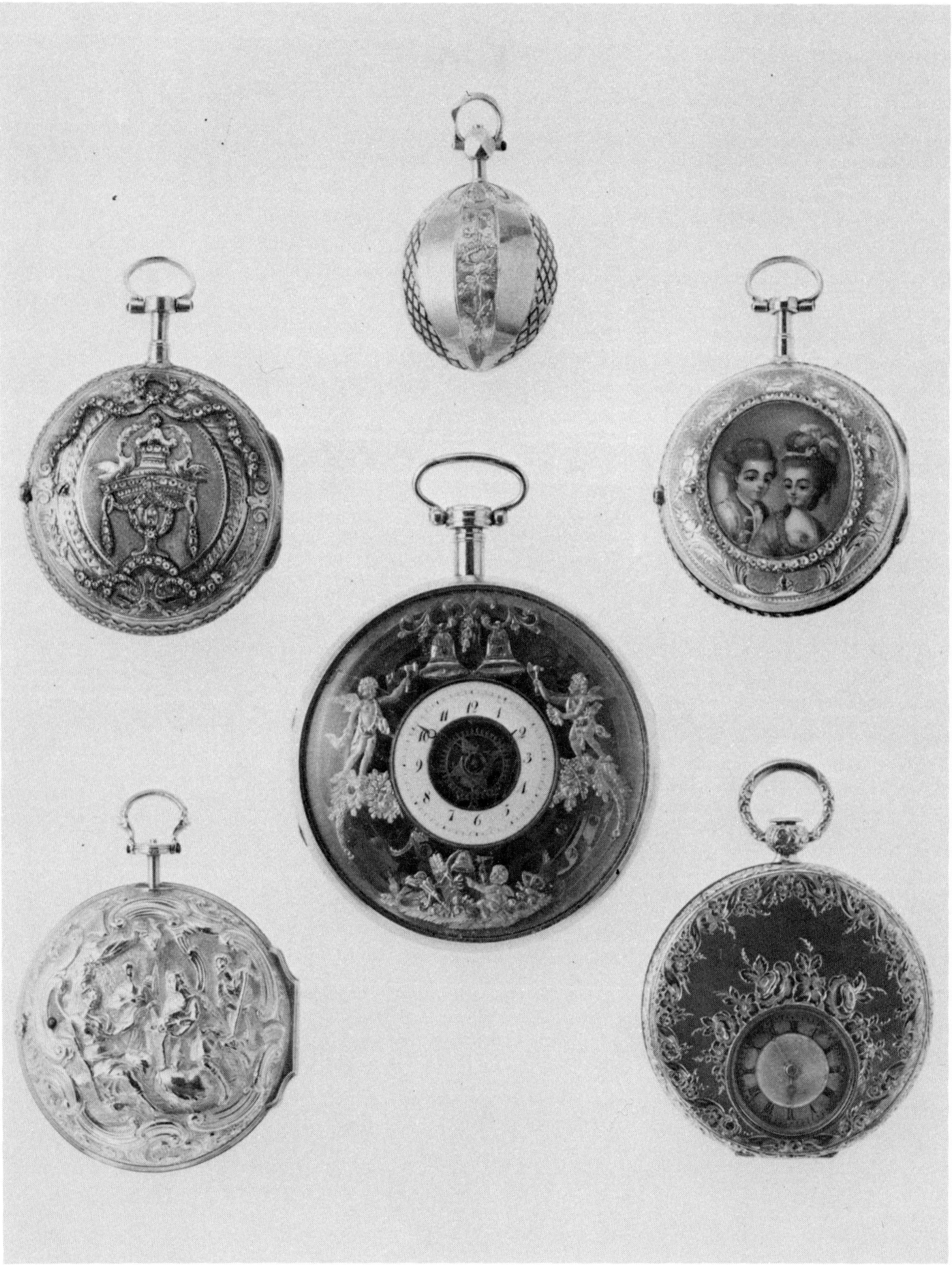

Collector's Gallery I

Swiss Gold and Enamel Melon Watch — Louis Duchene & Fils, Geneva — Circa 1790

Has verge movement and fusee. Movement and dial have signatures. Panels of chased geometric design and swags of flowers enamelled in pale blue, black, and white. Authors' Fair Price Estimate: $2,400.

Three-Color Gold Openface Watch — Charles Le Roy, Paris — Circa 1780

Verge movement. Roman numerals on white enamel dial set with stones. Hands also set with stones. Chased back with varicolored gold urn with two doves and surrounded by chased foliage and guilloche set with stones. Authors' Fair Price Estimate: $900.

Gold and Enamel Openface Watch — Mousson, Paris — Circa 1780

Verge movement; dial of white enamel. Bezel and hands are set with stones. Portrait of a young couple is enamelled on back. Border of engraved swags on matted ground. Authors' Fair Price Estimate: $800.

Swiss Gold Openface Automaton Watch — Maker unknown — Circa 1820

Small white enamel dial. Chased three-color gold putti strike bells with hammers in unison with the repeating. Emblems of love and cornucopiae surround the putti. The back is openwork chased with foliage. Authors' Fair Price Estimate: $3,000.

Gold Pair Case Watch — T. Miller, London, No. 8465 — Circa 1760

Verge movement and fusee. Roman numerals on white enamel dial. Blued steel beetle and poker hands. Plain first case hallmarked 1762, maker's mark T.R. Second case is repoussé and chased with Meleager offering the boar's head to Atalanta. Flowers and scrollwork surround the scene. Authors' Fair Price Estimate: $1,750.

Swiss Ultra-Thin Gold Openface Watch — Maker unknown — Circa 1835

Cylinder movement. Male key wind. Engine-turned silver dial at 6 o'clock. Front and back as well as inner cover are engine-turned and decorated with chased flowers. Chasing on pendant and bow. Authors' Fair Price Estimate: $3,000.

(above) **Swiss Gilt-Metal and Horn Openface Coach Watch with Alarm** — Dufour, Geneva — Circa 1790

Large verge movement and fusee. Alarm strikes on a bell. Elaborately pierced hands and short steel alarm hand. Arabic numerals on white enamel dial. Horn-covered case. The back shows a colorful scene of two dogs and a fisherman by a river with a tower and bridge in the background. Authors' Fair Price Estimate: $2,700.

(right) **Gilt-Metal Oval Watch** — Maker unknown — Case circa 1600, movement 19th century

The front case is pierced with a patera to reveal the numerals. The back is decorated with a pierced vase and flowering foliage and circled with borders of chevrons and leaves. Case was later fitted with verge movement. Gilt face is engraved. Back plate is decorated with scrollwork. Authors' Fair Price Estimate: $1,600.

Collector's Gallery I

Good English 18-Karat Gold Hunting Case Minute Repeating Chronograph — Ashley & Sims, 2 Green Terrace, Clerkenwell, No. 05247

Three-quarter plate lever movement, inscribed gold cuvette, slide repeat. Black Roman numerals on white enamel dial. Subsidiary dials for constant seconds and recorded minutes 1 to 60. Plain case with crest and motto engraved on front. Hallmarked 1902. Authors' Fair Price Estimate: $2,000.

German Gilt-Metal Drum-Shaped Clock Watch — Maker unknown — Circa 1575

Front pierced with chased therms, masks, and fruit. The back chased with therms, dolphins, and foliage. Band of pierced scrolling foliage with hounds pursuing a stag, hare, and two bears. The dial has Roman numerals I to XII and Arabic numerals 13 to 24. Touchpieces centered by strapwork enclose arabesques. Single blued steel hand with fleur-de-lys terminal. The movement is altered and converted, probably from stackfreed with 17th century cock. The fact that the Arabic numerals 13 to 19 are engraved in reverse and read 31, 41, 51, etc. adds some interest to this watch. Authors' Fair Price Estimate: $4,800.

Swiss Silver-Gilt and Enamel Openface Watch (made for the Oriental market) — Bovet, Fleurier, No. 920 — Early 19th century

Lever movement with elaborate gilt chasing, silver-gilt cuvette. White enamel dial with Roman numerals and sweep second hand. Signatures on dial and movement. Also Chinese signatures on movement and cuvette. The back is circled with pearls and is enamelled with a scene of a hunter on horseback pursuing a tiger. Gilding accents the bright colors. Pearls also adorn the pendant and bow. Authors' Fair Price Estimate: $3,500.

Swiss Gold and Enamel Openface Watch — Pierre Viala, Geneva — Circa 1790

Verge movement. Dial of white enamel has paste-set hands. The back is enamelled with the portrait of a woman on a blue enamel ground and set with pastes. The bezel is also decorated with pastes. Authors' Fair Price Estimate: $2,200.

Swiss Gold and Enamel Openface Lady's Watch — Maker unknown — Circa 1820

Verge movement; gold dial is engine-turned and has champlevé black enamel Roman numerals. The back is enamelled with a Cupid holding a cornucopia on a background of translucent blue enamel, surrounded with pearls. Authors' Fair Price Estimate: $500.

Viennese Silver-Gilt and Enamel Cushion-Shaped Watch — Maker unknown — Late 19th century

Verge movement; dial enamelled with cupids in a landscape. The inside is enamelled with a river scene. Andromeda and the monster are enamelled on the back. Authors' Fair Price Estimate: $1,000.

Swiss Silver-Gilt and Enamel Openface Chinese Duplex Watch — Maker unknown — Early 19th century

Movement of elaborately chased gilt. Dial of white enamel has Roman numerals and sweep second hand. A varicolored bouquet of flowers is enamelled on the back and circled with pearls. Authors' Fair Price Estimate: $3,000.

Swiss Gold and Enamel Openface Quarter Repeating Watch — Francois Alexandre Monnier, Geneva — Circa 1790

Verge movement repeating on a bell. Dial of white enamel with Arabic numerals and gold hand. The back is decorated with a chased urn and basket and two doves enamelled in white on a black background above an enamelled landscape with three figures. The band has two borders of leaves on a black background. The bezel is set with pearls. Outer case is of gilt metal with a glazed back. Authors' Fair Price Estimate: $1,700.

Swiss Gilt-Metal and Enamel Openface Watch — Pierre Viala, Geneva — Circa 1790

Verge movement; dial of white enamel with Arabic numerals. A classical female figure is enamelled on the back, framed by a chased grapevine enamelled in blue. Border of pearls and enamelled flowerheads alternate with borders of pastes. Authors' Fair Price Estimate: $750.

Collector's Gallery I 43

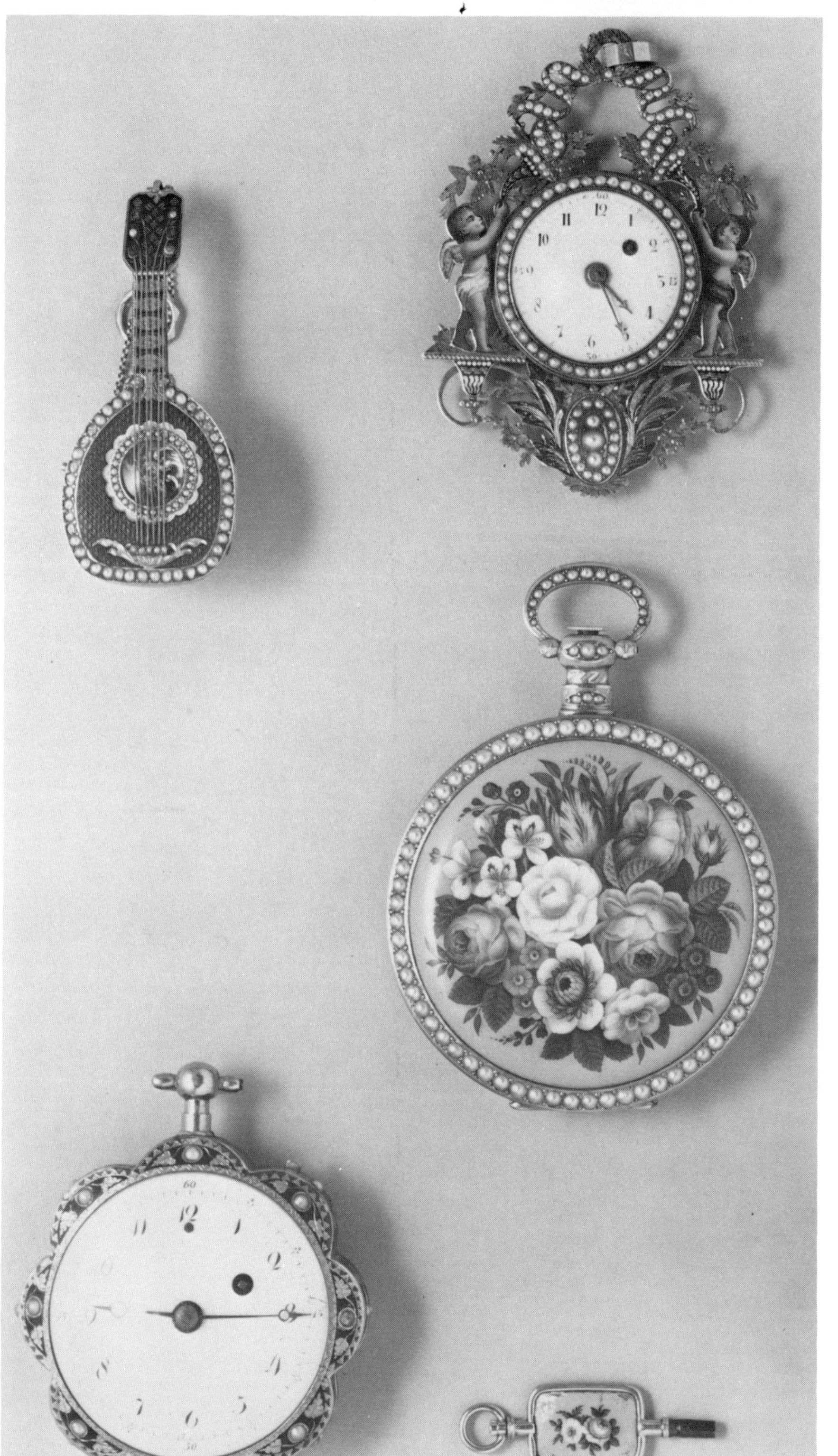

Collector's Gallery I

Opposite page
(top, left) **Swiss Gold and Enamel Mandolin Watch** — Maker unknown — Circa 1790

Verge movement and fusee. The front has a glazed panel which shows the balance. Decorative bands of translucent blue, opaque green, pale blue, and black enamel with geometric and foliate designs are bordered with split pearls. Strings and a pendant complete this very unusual watch. Authors' Fair Price Estimate: $4,000.

(top, right) **Swiss Gold and Enamel Pendant Watch** — Maker unknown — Circa 1810

Small verge movement. An openwork gold pendant, with two cherubs carrying cornucopiae of blue enamel surrounded by foliage and flowers of white and blue enamel, holds the dial. The pendant and dial as well as the patera mounted at the base are set with pearls. The back is painted with translucent blue enamel on a sun-ray ground. Authors' Fair Price Estimate: $5,000.

(bottom, left) **Fine Swiss Gold and Enamel Quarter Repeating Openface Watch** — Maker unknown — Circa 1800

Verge movement, quarter repeating on bell. Arabic numerals on white enamel dial. Chased octafoil case with reserves of leaves centered with pearls on grounds of black and blue enamel. A patera of blue enamel is mounted in center of back and set with graduated pearls and rose diamond on a background of translucent cranberry enamel over engine-turned ground of flowering plants. Authors' Fair Price Estimate: $3,500.

(bottom, right) **Swiss Gold and Enamel Openface Chinese Duplex Watch with Matching Key** — Circa 1810

Elaborately chased gilt movement. Glazed cuvette. Black Roman numerals on white enamel dial with sweep second hand. Back is enamelled with bouquet of flowers on a pale blue ground. Band is enamelled with garland of flowers and foliage. Border is set with split pearls. Enamelling and graduated pearls adorn pendant and bow. The key is enamelled with flowers on both sides to match. Authors' Fair Price Estimate: $8,800.

(right, top) **Swiss Gold and Enamel Pear Watch** — Circa 1790

Cylinder movement and fusee. Hands are missing. Curved panels of opaque green, primrose, and blue enamel interspaced with translucent orange reserves and chased sprays of leaves decorate the body. Pendant is decorated with filigreed leaves. Authors' Fair Price Estimate: $2,500.

(right, bottom) **Two-Color Gold and Enamel Pair Case Watch** — Berthoud, Paris — Circa 1785

Verge movement. Dial of white enamel. Back is painted with enamel showing two figures making an offering at a love altar with a sheep at one side and two doves above, all on ground of translucent blue enamel. Borders are chased with foliage. Outer case is plain with a glazed back. Authors' Fair Price Estimate: $2,800.

Swiss Gold Openface Skeletonized Watch with Silver and Enamel Chatelaine — Maker unknown — Late 18th century

The watch has skeletonized verge movement that is visible under the glazed back and bordered with an arrangement of scrolls set with pastes. The dial hands and band are also set with pastes. The chatelaine is formed of silver and translucent blue enamel panels set with jargoons. Authors' Fair Price Estimate: $1,500.

Collector's Gallery I

Swiss Gilt-Metal Openface Watch and Chatelaine — Maker unknown — Circa 1780

Has verge movement. Dial of white enamel. Bezel set with pastes. The back is chased with two doves and a pedestal before an arch set with pastes. The chatelaine is chased with urns and flowers. The top panel is decorated with a chased love trophy and hung with a fish pendant and vinaigrette, probably of a later date. Authors' Fair Price Estimate: $800.

Gilt-Metal and Rock Crystal Octagonal Watch — Probably Swiss — Early 17th century

Has verge movement, fusee, and gut. The balance cock is in the shape of a foliage spray and pinned to the foot. Dial is engraved with scrolling foliage and flowers and centered with a city view. Single blued steel hand. The movement is secured in the case by a pair of springs. The case has engraved borders of leaves and is mounted with beveled rock crystal panels. The swiveling shaped and chased pendant has a baluster finial. Authors' Fair Price Estimate: $6,200.

Now we have all the power we need inside the barrel, and we attach a ratchet wheel to the barrel arbor to store up the power inside the barrel. When the ratchet wheel is rotated, it turns the arbor and winds up the attached spring. Since the mainspring is exerting its force against the ratchet wheel, a "click" is used to engage the teeth of the ratchet wheel, to keep it moving only in the winding direction. As we have seen, winding was not done, in early times, with the winding button or crown as it is done today. However, if you simply understand the present method, the older ones will become apparent as you study them. The ratchet wheel is turned by a set of gears connecting to the winding crown, or more correctly, to a stem connected to the crown. These gears are called the winding mechanism and when the crown and stem are turned, the stem, whose other end is inserted into the clutch wheel, turns this wheel also.

Just above the clutch wheel is the winding pinion which is, in turn, revolved by the clutch wheel. The winding pinion's radial teeth then mesh with the winding wheel which is at right angles to it and directly behind the stem in the back of the movement. This combined action winds the watch.

All the average person does with a watch is wind and set it. We have detailed only the winding aspect of the watch because, again, there is only time within a book such as this for the broad picture. Any library is well stocked with books on watch making and repair that explain the operation of a watch in full detail. We will discuss that operation here in as nondetailed a sweep as possible.

We now have the mainspring wound. Remember the early problems that arose. A mainspring that is newly wound pulled much harder than when it was nearly run down. The stackfreed, previously discussed, was the first effort to correct the problem and worked to some extent. Then came the fusee which did a much better job. The fusee was used into the nineteenth century until it was no longer needed. Mainsprings were made of better steel, and they were made longer so that only a portion of their length was used, and variations of strength could, thus, be greatly lessened. The old verge escapement was replaced with escapements much less sensitive to driving power change. The hairspring was developed. All these developments took years, decades, centuries to develop.

The mainspring and barrel drive, called the "train," consists of four wheels: the center wheel, the third wheel and pinion, the fourth wheel and pinion, and the escape wheel and pinion. It is the train's job to supply energy to the escapement, but it does this in small doses. If the mainspring's power was sent directly to the escapement without rationing by the train, the power outlay would be something for a little watch. And the power would be so quickly used up, rewinding would become almost a constant chore. A watch today can run for forty hours. The earliest watches did well to go fifteen hours, with twelve hours probably the norm.

There are three parts to the escapement: the escape wheel, the pallet, and the balance. The escapement can be called the brain of the watch. It controls the flow of power through the wheels so that all turn with a steady rate of speed. All sorts of improvements have been made through the years in all areas of escapements. No effort will be made to cover them all.

Typical mechanism of a repeater watch.

What Makes a Watch Tick

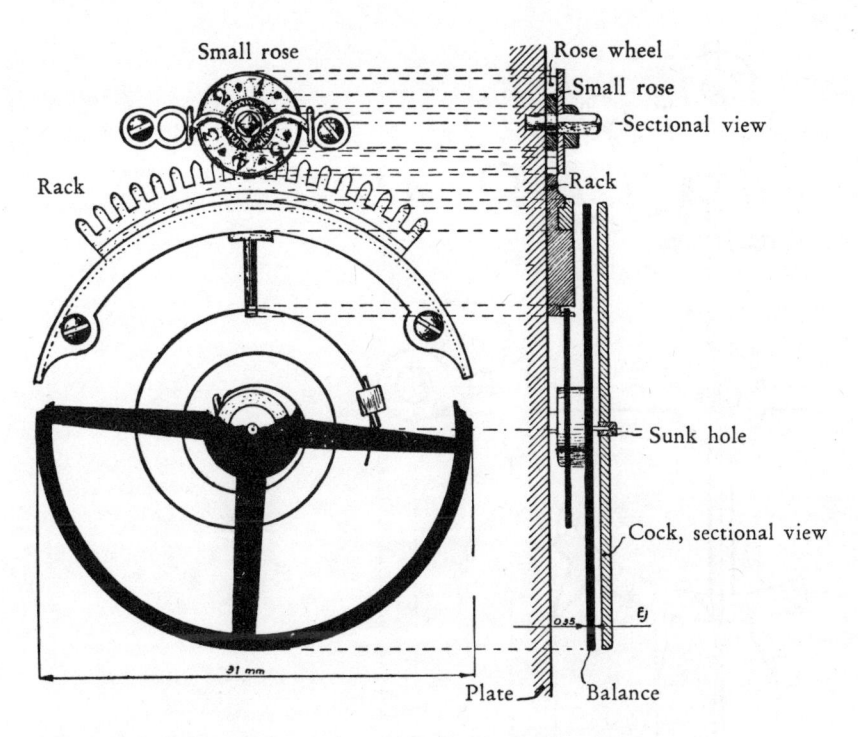

Large balance watch by Jean-Louis Trembley, Geneva, circa 1700, showing the regulating device of 18th century watches.

Most important of all was the invention of the balance spring. This mechanism or hairspring, as it is also known, did not exist until watches were almost two hundred years old. The motions of the balance were not controlled save when a straight hog's bristle was occasionally used, and then, not with the greatest results in the world. We can give credit to Hooke, Hautefeuille, and Huygens for the invention of the balance spring. Later Breguet improved the balance spring with the overcoil. Balance springs were flat coils, but Breguet brought up the outer end over the rest of the coils. Among other things, there was now less danger that the coils would get caught in the regulator pin because the watch was dropped or even jarred.

Usually the balance and hairspring vibrate back and forth 18,000 times an hour, or 300 times a minute, or 5 times a second. In other words, while the balance is moving, the watch is actually at rest until the balance unlocks the escapement. As the escape wheel moves, the second hand

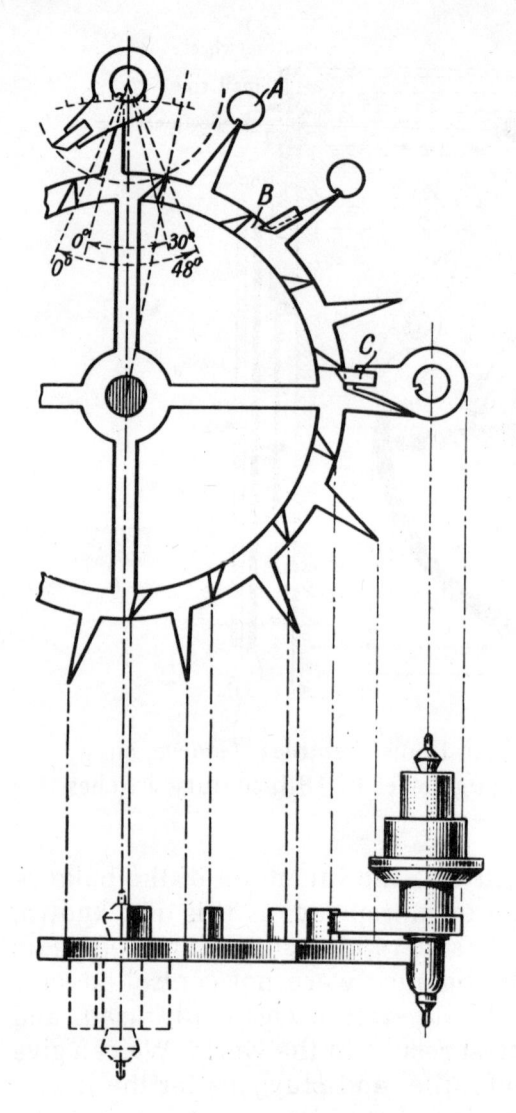

Saunier's duplex escapement with (A) the ruby roller, (B) drop of escape wheel onto the impulse pallet (C).

of the fourth wheel moves forward just one-fifth of a second. Five escapes are needed to make the second hand move one full second on its dial.

For a watch to indicate the time, the hour, and the minute, the dial train is needed. It is composed of three main parts: the cannon pinion, the minute wheel and pinion, and the hour wheel. They are situated under the dial, and they power the hour and minute hands.

The indicating mechanism is, of course, the hands and dial of the watch. There is also the setting mechanism which is the connecting link between the dial train and the winding mechanism. The setting mechanism is composed of a series of levers that make it possible to set the hands through the crown and the stem.

Early watches had only one dial which was the hour hand. The minute hand became widely used at the beginning of the eighteenth century. It was made possible by improvements that made watches more accurate—namely, better escapements and jewels. There were minute hands before that time, but they were merely the single work of

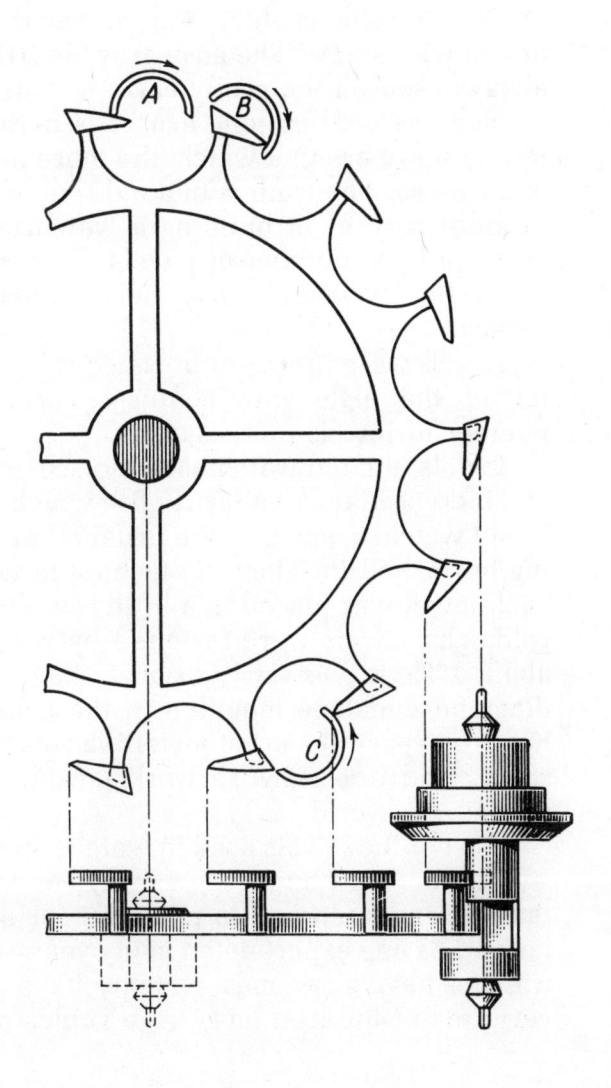

Saunier's cylinder or horizontal escapement with (A) showing impulse and (B) inside locking and (C) outside locking.

some able watchmaker, hardly something that could be put in general use. These early minute hands were not concentric. When the concentric minute hand was developed, it allowed the hour hand to be driven by the minute hand, and it allowed for easy setting of the hands. Once accuracy was further improved, it was possible to add the second hand.

Dials of old watches were works of art. Made of gold, silver or brass, they often bore chased or engraved decorations. Many dials were painted in enamel. The plain white enamel dial was introduced about 1700. Until quite recent times, Roman numerals were used with the bottoms generally towards the center; thus, some were what we would consider upside down.

Which watch is older? One whose dial has a IIII for a 4, or one with an IV? The answer is the IIII, which was almost always used on the really early watches.

Now, as well as long ago, it is believed that the more jewels there are in a watch, the more accurate it is. That is and isn't so. The truth is that old-time watchmakers tended to more careful in building a watch movement that contained a large number of jewels compared to one that contained few; so in that sense, more jewels did mean more accuracy.

Jewels were first used in watches by Facio at the beginning of the eighteenth century. Through the years, the number of jewels increased.

Jewels, the old watchmakers discovered, cut the friction and increased the regularity with which a watch would run. In old watches, jewels were fastened in watch plates by being burnished in. Then the technique was changed so that each jewel was placed in a little round setting of low-karat gold. The jewels were fastened by two tiny screws. From about 1725, it was fairly usual to have a reasonably sized diamond endstone mounted in the cock. For close to one hundred years, the art of jewelling was basically an English secret, and finer English workmanship gained acceptance around the world.

Most of the jewels used in watches were not very expensive at all. A few hundred years ago and more recently than that, a gentleman had to pay a lot for a watch with costly jewels. As one expert noted many years ago, "Very common watches have glass, most watches have garnets, and only a very few of the best ones have rubies and sapphires."

Chapter VI
America and Other Late Comers in Watches

There are antique American watches, but they are late ones, mostly produced after 1850. As *Britten's*, the great, venerable, reference volume on clocks and watches states, "America cannot be said to have had a watchmaking industry before 1830." Well, there really was—of sorts.

There were watches in colonial days so there must have been some watchmakers. Whether they were full time at it is another matter. Remember that watches in the early seventeenth century were really pieces of jewelry and could belong only to the very wealthy. When production boomed in England after 1675, there were some more reasonably priced watches, and some of these were brought to the colonies.

It is conceivable that a number of watches were assembled in America in early colonial days, but they were probably made completely of parts constructed in England. A man who repaired watches would order extra parts, and every once in a while, he might put a bunch of parts together and make a watch.

There is some written record of a "Thom. Stretch, Phila." having turned out at least twenty-five watches long before the American Revolution, but there seems to have been no watch surviving that could be analyzed to determine if it was a homemade product or one assembled in this country.

Naturally, all the early clock and watchmakers in America came from England and Holland. They had learned their trade there, come to America with the tools they had used there, and worked on watches they were familiar with. Perhaps they sold jewelry or did locksmithing work, as well as sell and repair watches and clocks. In any event a number of watchmakers turn up in the very late eighteenth century in cities and towns in New York, New Jersey, Massachusetts, Delaware, Pennsylvania, Connecticut, and Rhode Island.

By this time, some watches do appear to be of local

manufacture although most still smack of being made entirely of English parts.

The first recognized maker of watches in America was Thomas Harland who set up a primitive sort of clock and watch factory in Norwich, Connecticut. Harland had been born in England and had come to Boston. Not much is known of his Boston days, but he must have been involved there in clocks and watches. By 1775 Harland was at work in Norwich where he became a very prosperous tradesman, as well as a clock and watchmaker. The records indicate that he had as many as ten or twelve people working for him at one time. Norwich, at the time, was a bustling seaport and could have supported a clock and watchmaker. Therefore, while some of Harland's employees worked as sellers, some must have been involved in watchmaking. Harland probably produced about forty clocks a year and somewhere between two and two hundred watches. This hardly indicates that watchmaking had really taken hold. Harland's ads declared he made "horizontal, repeating, and plain watches in gold, silver, metal, or covered cases."

The plain watches Harland sold were of the common verge type, and some of them survive to the present. The horizontal watches are the newer cylinder escapement ones, and if Harland made and sold many of them, none apparently have come down to us. Harland worked at his trade in Norwich for more than thirty years until 1806. One of Harland's apprentices was Daniel Burnap (1759-1838) who eventually set up in business in East Windsor. He was recognized as a fine craftsman, and a number of his clocks rank as among the best of this early period. He too was into watches to some extent, but his activities lean much more to clocks.

After Harland the next important watchmaker was probably Luther Goddard. He went into the watchmaking business on quite a large scale, from 1809 to 1817. Goddard attempted to take advantage of the Jefferson Embargo which limited the importing of watches, among other things, from abroad. It is believed that Goddard worked as an apprentice in Grafton, Massachusetts, but there is no proof of this. His original calling was that of a clergyman, and how and why he switched to watchmaking is not clear. But the embargo offered Goddard a golden opportunity. He set himself up in Shrewsbury, Massachusetts, in 1809 and began turning out watches. They were of the standard English verge type. As long as he could get English parts, Goddard turned out quite a respectable product. Goddard did start making many of his own parts. Many of his balance cocks were his own, though not of the usual English design but pierced and engraved with the trusty American Eagle. All in all, Goddard turned out more than five hundred movements which means he probably had a fair number of employees.

Watch critics might find many of Goddard's watches slightly below the best in workmanship, but remember the obstacles under which he worked. Parts were hard to come by, and he and his assistants were really sort of provincial workmen starting an industry in a none-too-rich land that wanted quality—and low prices. Judged on that basis, Goddard's works were extremely good. Nonetheless, Goddard was forced out of business in 1817. The lifting of the embargo did it for there was no way a primitive plant in Massachusetts was going to compete with the techniques of an industry that was centuries old in England. The flood of English watches were better made and cheaper, and Goddard was a beaten man. He cut his losses and returned to preaching the gospel. Along with his ministerial chores, however, Goddard continued to repair watches up until his death in 1842.

After Goddard gave up the fight, a few other American watchmakers attempted to do battle with the English. There was Jacob Custer in Norristown, Pennsylvania, and W.E. Harper in Philadelphia. They had to turn out lever escapement watches because the verge was now finished. Both men did some nice work, but they were incapable of producing any great number of watches because the English competition was too stiff.

The really gallant try was made by the four Pitkin Brothers of Hartford, Connecticut.Of them, the two most important in watchmaking were James and Henry. Most of the Pitkin boys apprenticed with Jacob Sargeant, a Hartford silversmith and clockmaker. Henry clearly proved the most talented. He was also a young man obsessed. His dream was to produce the first truly all-American watch, one that would top in quality anything being imported from England.

Henry realized that this would require the principle of mass production, and in this sense he was the forerunner of Henry Ford in this country.

The Pitkin brothers bought out Sargeant on his retirement, and Henry was immersed working out watch designs and machines on which they could be built. The first Pitkin watch was produced in 1838 and was an artistic and a financial success. However, there was other trouble brewing, and the brothers split up with Henry and James moving to New York and setting themselves up in the watch business. Henry was continually obsessed with beating the English, and as the brothers had many disappointments and their business suffered pitfalls, his mind started to be affected. During this time, the Pitkins turned out about eight hundred to one thousand watches of really fine quality. Only three hundred were ever sold. Many of the others were destroyed by Henry Pitkin in one of his fits of insane rages. Others disappeared. Finally, in 1846, Henry committed suicide.

Even before Henry's death, James Pitkin was forced to sell the business. However, the Pitkin brothers had started something. They had failed, but their assets were taken over by men who would take watchmaking in America to a new and higher stage. These men would later become known as pioneers in the development of the post-1850 American watch, its golden years. They proved more successful than Henry Pitkin, but they benefited from his mantle. They were the fathers of the American watch if success is standard of judgement. But there are those who insist the credit must go to Henry Pitkin. He laid the plans for the way the American watch would have to develop. It was his machinery that his successor used to produce the great American watch. If Henry Pitkin is to be judged a failure, he was the most magnificent failure in the annals of watchmaking.

The men who bought out the Pitkins business were two remarkable men in their own right, Aaron L. Dennison and Edward Howard. Like Henry Pitkin they, too, were dreamers, long on dreams and short on cash. Not that they were poor—they had been high bidders on the Pitkin equipment—but they were thinking on a big scale and big money was needed.

Dennison and Howard were close friends and inevitable

America and Other Late Comers in Watches 59

Plain Polished.
New, small model; flat bow.

No.		Open Face.	Hunting.
L 520	WATCH CASE ONLY.	$6.50	$10.90

Fitted complete with the following movements:

L 520A	Swiss, 7 J., nickel...	16.50	20.90
L 521	Swiss, 15 J., nickel...	19.60	24.00
L 522	Swiss, 17 J., nickel...	22.75	27.15
L 523	Hamp., 15 J., nickel..	26.60	31.00
L 524	Elg., 15 J., nickel...	27.10	31.50
L 525	Wal., 15 J., nickel...	31.15	35.65
L 526	Elg., 17 J., nickel...	31.90	36.30
L 527	Wal., 17 J., nickel...	37.10	41.50
L 528	Wal., 17 J., adjusted nickel	44.35	48.75
L 529	Wal. Riverside, 19 J., adjusted	75.85	80.25

Engraving 3 letter monogram, as illustrated $3.00 EXTRA.

Engine Turned.
New, small model; flat bow.

No.		Open Face.	Hunting.
L 531	WATCH CASE ONLY.	$6.50	$10.90

Fitted complete with the following movements:

L 531A	Swiss, 7 J., nickel...	16.50	20.90
L 532	Swiss, 15 J., nickel...	19.60	24.00
L 533	Swiss, 17 J., nickel...	22.75	27.15
L 534	Hamp., 15 J., nickel..	26.60	31.00
L 535	Elg., 15 J., nickel...	27.10	31.50
L 536	Wal., 15 J., nickel...	31.15	35.65
L 537	Elg., 17 J., nickel...	31.90	36.30
L 538	Wal., 17 J., nickel...	37.10	41.50
L 539	Wal., 17 J., adjusted nickel	44.35	48.75
L 540	Wal. Riverside, 19 J., nickel	75.85	80.25

Engraved, Shield Center.
New, small model; flat bow.

No.		Open Face.	Hunting.
L 542	WATCH CASE ONLY.	$7.25	$12.20

Fitted complete with the following movements:

L 542A	Swiss, 7 J., nickel...	17.25	22.20
L 543	Swiss, 15 J., nickel...	20.35	25.30
L 544	Swiss, 17 J., nickel...	23.50	28.45
L 545	Hamp., 15 J., nickel..	27.35	32.30
L 546	Elg., 15 J., nickel...	27.85	32.80
L 547	Wal., 15 J., nickel...	31.90	36.95
L 548	Elg., 17 J., nickel...	32.65	37.60
L 549	Wal., 17 J., nickel...	37.85	42.80
L 550	Wal., 17 J., adjusted nickel	45.10	50.05
L 551	Wal. Riverside, 19 J., adjusted	76.60	81.55

Fancy Engraved.
New, small model; flat bow.

No.		Open Face.	Hunting.
L 553	WATCH CASE ONLY.	$7.25	$12.20

Fitted complete with the following movements:

L 553A	Swiss, 7 J., nickel...	17.25	22.20
L 554	Swiss, 15 J., nickel...	20.35	25.30
L 555	Swiss, 17 J., nickel...	23.50	28.45
L 556	Hamp., 15 J., nickel..	27.35	32.30
L 557	Elg., 15 J., nickel...	27.85	32.80
L 558	Wal., 15 J., nickel...	31.90	36.95
L 559	Elg., 17 J., nickel...	32.65	37.60
L 560	Wal., 17 J., nickel...	37.85	42.80
L 561	Wal., 17 J., adjusted nickel	45.10	50.05
L 562	Wal. Riverside, 19 J., adjusted nickel	76.60	81.55

Fancy Engraved.
New, small model; flat bow.

No.		Open Face.	Hunting.
L 564	WATCH CASE ONLY.	$7.25	$12.20

Fitted complete with the following movements:

L 564A	Swiss, 7 J., nickel...	17.25	22.20
L 565	Swiss, 15 J., nickel...	20.35	25.30
L 566	Swiss, 17 J., nickel...	23.50	28.45
L 567	Hamp., 15 J., nickel..	27.35	32.30
L 568	Elg., 15 J., nickel...	27.85	32.80
L 569	Wal., 15 J., nickel...	31.90	36.95
L 570	Elg., 17 J., nickel...	32.65	37.60
L 571	Wal., 17 J., nickel...	37.85	42.80
L 572	Wal., 17 J., adjusted nickel	45.10	50.05
L 573	Wal. Riverside, 19 J., adjusted nickel	76.60	81.55

Fancy Engraved.
New, small model; flat bow.

No.		Open Face.	Hunting.
L 575	WATCH CASE ONLY.	$7.25	$12.20

Fitted complete with the following movements:

L 575A	Swiss, 7 J., nickel...	17.25	22.20
L 576	Swiss, 15 J., nickel...	20.35	25.30
L 577	Swiss, 17 J., nickel...	23.50	28.45
L 578	Hamp., 15 J., nickel..	27.35	32.30
L 579	Elg., 15 J., nickel...	27.85	32.80
L 580	Wal., 15 J., nickel...	31.90	36.95
L 581	Elg., 17 J., nickel...	32.65	37.60
L 582	Wal., 17 J., nickel...	37.85	42.80
L 583	Wal., 17 J., adjusted nickel	45.10	50.05
L 584	Wal. Riverside, 19 J., adjusted nickel	76.60	81.55

Watches with 1915 retail prices are all now worth ten times or more their original prices.

business partners because they thought the same way. Historians have had trouble determining which of the two came up with which idea first, mainly because they seemed to come up with the same ideas. The basic ones were that watches, to be produced successfully in America, would require factory methods as opposed to individual hand crafting. They wanted to use automatic machinery, and most important, they wanted to have absolute interchangeability of parts.

Dennison often visited the United States Armory at Springfield where rifles were being produced on the mass methods and interchangeable plans started by Eli Whitney. Howard, like Dennison, had apprenticed as a clock and watchmaker and was also very taken with the mass method of production. However, he thought the principle might best be applied to the making of locomotives. According to the tale, which may be aprocryphal, Dennison dissuaded him on locomotives and into watches instead. Both knew their business and were good at it. They were even better in their dreams.

Dennison later recalled: "The principal thinking up of the matter was done when I was in the business at the corner of Bromfield and Washington Streets in Boston. Many a night after I had done a good day's work at the store, and a good evening's work at home, repairing watches for personal friends, I used to stroll out upon the 'Common' and give my mind full play upon this project, and, as far as I can recollect what my plans then were as to system and methods to be employed, they are identical with those in existence in the principal watch factories at the present time."

And Howard writes: "One difficulty I found was that watchmaking did not exist in the United States as an industry. There were watchmakers so called, at that time, and there are great numbers of the same kind now, but they never made a watch; their business being only to clean and repair. I knew from experience that there was no proper system employed in making watches. The work was all done by hand ... As I say, all of these minute parts were laboriously cut and filed out by hand, so that it will be readily understood that in watches purporting to be of the same size and of the same makers, there were no two alike, and there was no interchangeability of parts. Consequently, it was 'cut and try.' A great deal of time was wasted and many imperfections resulted. The development of the plan (to use automatic machinery) was the result of long thinking."

There matters stood around the middle of the nineteenth century. Dennison and Howard had some of the Pitkin machinery and plenty of plans for more. They were both successful clockmakers, but now they needed a lot of capital, more than either possessed. Raising capital for the making of American watches was no easy task. There was a lot of prejudice against the idea. Many felt the English would never be beaten, and the fact that Henry Pitkin had killed himself was not the greatest money-raising pitch. Even their close friends started to ridicule them.

Finally, however, they found an angel. He was Samuel Curtis of Boston who put up $20,000 to get the project started. It was a very large sum of money in those days, and that $20,000 probably did more than any sum of money ever expended to establish the American watch industry. Curtis was not a watchmaker. He was more like the Broadway angel who stepped in and saved the show with his money. He did, and there now was enough capital to form the American Horologe Company. After a string of other names, this became the Waltham Watch Company.

Dennison was sent to England to study watchmaking techniques there and to obtain regular supplies for the new venture. What impressed Dennison the most about production methods was the very thorough division of labor. Each man, an expert in his specialty, worked on one particular aspect of the production process. Since this was intricate work, it did not create the dangerous boredom that was to develop in more mundane production lines. Dennison came back with nothing but praise for the systems he studied. But he had plans for improvements.

The first factory of the American Horologe Company was built in Roxbury, and by August, 1850, they had produced their first watch. It was fullplate, 18-size (generally the largest size made for men) and it ran for eight days. However, it was not much of a success. The required mainspring was too long. It was cumbersome. The model was dropped and a thirty-six-hour watch was substituted. It was ready for the market in the spring of 1853. By the time it came out, the name of the company had been changed to the Warren Manufacturing Company, to honor a Revolutionary War hero who had lived in Roxbury. By the time the first one hundred watches were issued, carrying the name of Warren, the company's name was changed again, this time to the Boston Watch Company. The next seven hundred or so watches turned out now bore the name "Samuel Curtis" in honor of the financial angel whose backing had made it all possible.

Such history is important to collectors because they know if they run across a watch named Warren, they have one of the first one hundred watches produced by what was later to be called the Waltham Watch Company, Similarly, to happen across a Samuel Curtis means it is from the next batch of seven hundred watches.

The watches sold for $40 and were very much English in style. The first watches used the ratchet-tooth escape wheel which is typical English work. Dennison and Howard soon changed this to the club-tooth style. Production had not been easy. Howard once wrote: "We did not know how to make a jewel, or a dial, or to do proper gilding, or to produce a mirror polish on steel. We had to invent all the tools to make the different parts. After being designed or invented, they had to be made in the factory by our own machinists in order to have them perfect and durable."

But despite such problems, the new watches were a success, so much so the factory was now too small, and living accomodations around Roxbury were not good enough to attract good watch workers. A decision was made to build a new factory in Waltham, Massachusetts. By this time, the company had about ninety workers and was producing five watches a day. The watch movements were now being engraved "Dennison, Howard, and Davis." D.P. Davis was Howard's partner in his original clock business.

When the new factory was completed in the fall of 1854, production was up to an astounding six watches a day. But then things started going wrong. Being innovative men, both Dennison and Howard were rather pleased to have the new factory built with poured concrete, an innovative process in its own right at the time. All sorts of problems developed with the concrete, and production was disrupted.

Even worse was the fact that the sale of watches general-

D. A. A. Buck's long-winding Waterbury Watch, made in 1882 and later. The first successful popular-priced watch.

These Waterbury watches sold for about four dollars each, roughly one-fourth of competitive prices. As the demand grew, the new Waterbury Watch Company was formed in 1880. Outgrowing the old plant, it built a new factory in Waterbury in 1882-83. A description sounds quite up to date: walls of windows, high ceilings, good ventilation and heat, well lighted, neat and clean—now a proud tradition for factories in the industry.

In 1884, "over 300 operators, many of whom were women, tended the automatic machines in comfort," making six hundred watches a day. Here was the first generation of highly skilled women operators who still continue to make their important contribution to the production of American timepieces.

Reproduction of an early newspaper advertisement (circa 1895) for a classic timepiece.

ly fell way off. The factory had been very expensive to build, and Dennison and Howard were constantly experimenting with new processes that cost heavily in time and money. Tooling up with a tremendous amount of automatic machinery was an additional drain.

And through this all, Howard insisted on a standard of excellence in the watches being produced. Some critics said he should compromise just a bit to help the company in this period of economic travail, but he ignored all such suggestions.

By the spring of 1857, the company was on its knees, and finally it was sold for $56,000. The buyer was the Philadelphia watch-case-making firm of Tracy, Baker & Co. The "new" firm name of the watch company became Tracy, Baker & Co. Dennison was kept on as superintendent while Howard returned to Roxbury and started anew in watchmaking. "I had to begin at the bottom and make all tools anew," he stated later. "I returned to my old factory at Roxbury, and founded a new company with the understanding that I was to have my own way about the quality of watches that bore the name of Howard."

Howard's company went on to become the much respected E. Howard Watch Works of Waltham. And Tracy, Baker & Co. did not last long. Soon both Baker and Tracy bowed out, and the firm ended up in the control of Royal E. Robbins who proved to be the dynamic personality the business needed. He advertised heavily, and some of his advertising methods are still studied today. Robbins added several less expensive watch lines with cheaper ones having only seven jewels.

Economic conditions got worse, however, and for a while Robbins, too, appeared doomed. However, he managed to survive by merging his company with others. It was then called the American Watch Company and proved very viable. With the outbreak of the Civil War in 1861, Robbins was forced to retrench further although he did bring out the first lady's watch made in this country. It was 10-size and had a key wind.

Robbins was the first watchmaker to see the Civil War as a boon for watches. He correctly concluded there would be a huge market for a reasonably priced watch for the military and he started turning it out. Robbins made a tremendous amount of money for the company and in 1866 a cash *(right)* **Gold Pair Case Watch with Gold and Gilt-Metal Chatelaine** — Pierre Dupont, London, 1759

Verge movement with a white enamel dial with black Roman numerals. The first case is hallmarked London 1759; the second case is repoussé and chased with classical figures within scrollwork and flowers. The gold chatelaine is pierced with rococo scrollwork. Authors' Fair Price Estimate: $2,000.

(below, left) **Swiss White Gold, Diamond, and Enamel Ball Watch and Brooch** — Circa 1900

The watch is decorated with translucent grey enamel overlaid with a pierced design set with tiny diamonds, suspended from a hook-form brooch also set with diamonds. Authors' Fair Price Estimate: $750.

(below, right) **Gold, Sapphire, and Diamond Lapel Watch and Brooch**

The small circular watch covered by a hinged openwork design set with five diamonds and four sapphires, suspended from a matching scrolled arrangement of openwork gold set with eleven sapphires and nine diamonds; the watch by Tissot. Authors' Fair Price Estimate: $750.

Swiss Openface Watch with Skeletonized Scenic Movement — Maker unknown — Circa 1860

Lever movement has key wind. The plates are pierced, engraved, and partly gilt with an infant bacchanal holding cup and standing on the back of a leopard, surrounded with vines and flowers. Engine-turned silver dial has chased gold decoration. Has later gold exhibition case. Authors' Fair Price Estimate: $500.

German Gilt-Metal Watch Case — Circa 1570

Of drum shape, the sides pierced and chased with an elaborate hunting scene repeated on the base within a laurel border and surrounding a medallion of Science. The cover pierced with, caryatids in alternating designs between borders of running foliage and fruit with iron masks at intervals. Authors' Fair Price Estimate: $900.

Collector's Gallery II   67

(above) **German Gilt-Metal Watch Case** — Circa 1570

Of drum shape, the sides pierced and chased with a procession of putti and horses. The cover, centered by a cast and chased scene of the Nativity, the base with the Crucifixion; both surrounded by strapwork and on the base, winged cherub heads. Authors' Fair Price Estimate: $800.

(right) **Swiss Openface Musical Watch** — Circa 1900.

Plays two tunes, one identifiable as "Amaryllis," on a cylinder on the hour or at will. Small eccentric white enamel chapter ring on a pink dial enamelled *en grisaille* with a music trophy and a spray of foliage. The case is partly silvered and partly gilt. Authors' Fair Price Estimate: $1,250.

(left, top) **Swiss Gilt-Metal and Enamel Openface Watch** — Maker unknown — Circa 1800

Has verge movement. Dial of white enamel. Bezel set with pastes. Back is enamelled with a young girl and a begging dog. An open birdcage is at one side. Authors' Fair Price Estimate: $300.

(left, bottom) **Swiss Gilt-Metal and Enamel Openface Watch** — Soret, Geneva — Circa 1790

Verge movement. The dial is of white enamel. Borders are set with pastes. The back is enamelled with two lovers in a pastoral scene. Sun rays are chased above them. Authors' Fair Price Estimate: $500.

Opposite page
(top, right) **Swiss Gilt-Metal and Enamel Openface Watch** — Deroche, Geneva — Circa 1790

Verge movement. Bezel and hands set with pastes. A young couple in a landscape is painted on the back. Authors' Fair Price Estimate: $500.

(left) **English Triple Case Watch for the South American Market** — Signed Higgs y Evans, Londres, No. 27416 — 1810

Verge movement has pierced foliate pillars and silver dust cap. White enamel dial has blued steel beetle and poker hands. Two silver cases are hallmarked London 1810. The outer case is covered in tortoiseshell painted with a woman strolling with a parasol, dog, and a blackamoor attendant on the grounds of a country house. Has silver chain and metal key, circa 1830. Authors' Fair Price Estimate: $700.

(bottom, right) **Gilt-Metal and Enamel Openface Watch** — Signed Le Roy à Paris — Circa 1800

Has verge movement. White enamel dial has gold hands. Back is enamelled with two lovers in a landscape with roses, surrounded by blue and white enamel flowers and leaves. Authors' Fair Price Estimate: $600.

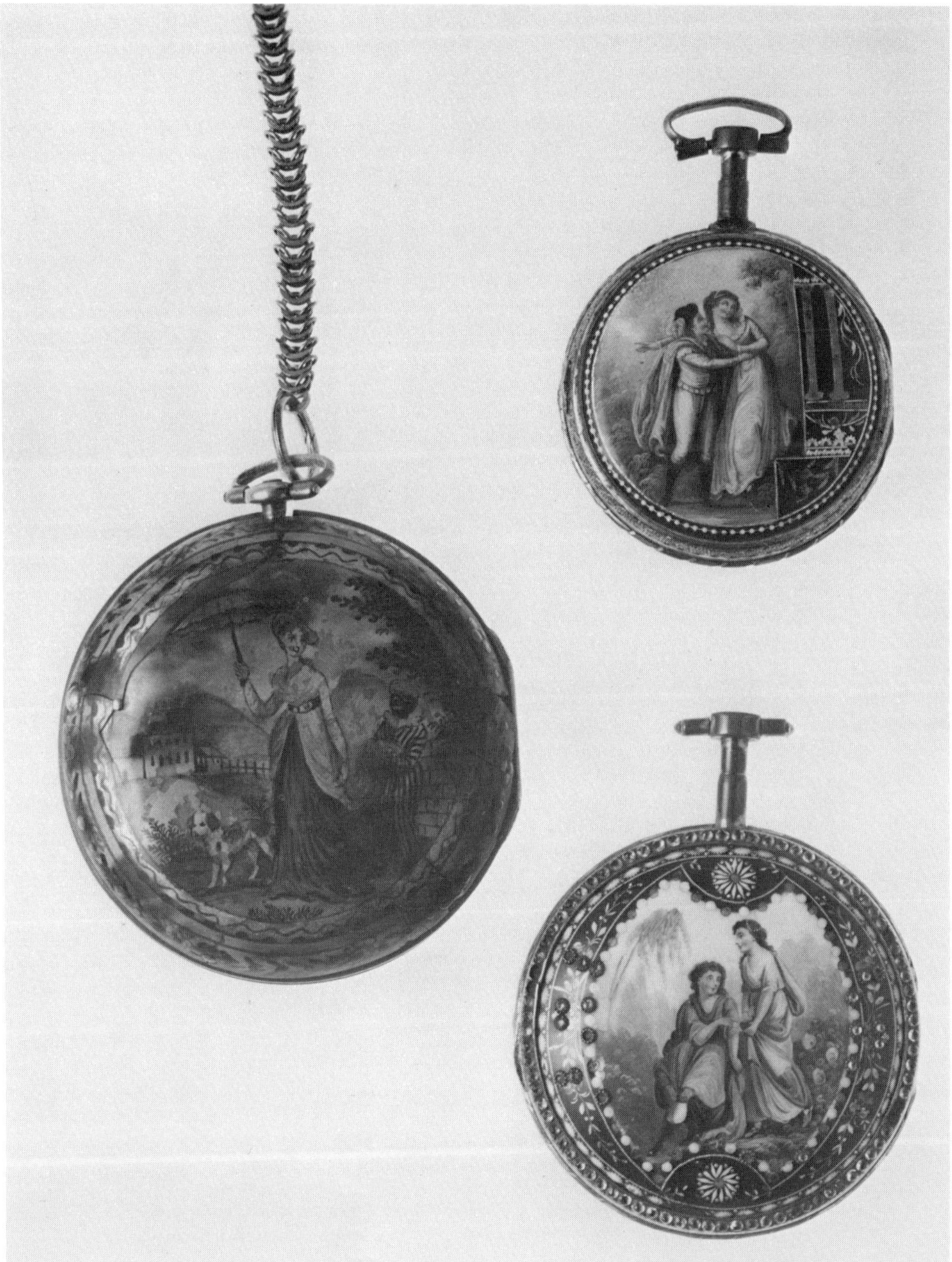

(above) **Interesting Marine Chronometer** — Edward Baker, London, No. 1080 — Circa 1840

Detent escapement, free-sprung. Silvered dial with black Roman numerals, naval insignia, and blued steel hands. Subsidiary seconds dial and fifty-six-hour up-and-down scale. Mounted in gimbals in mahogany case with maker's name and number. Glazed inner cover. Has ratchet key. Was purchased for naval use in 1842 and served time on the following ships: H.M.S. Gannet, 1866-1868; H.M.S. Mymidon, 1884-1888; H.M.S. Narcissus, 1892-1895; H.M.S. Brilliant, 1896; H.M.S. Rinaldo, 1901-1905. This chronometer was also lent to the expedition to observe the Transit of Venus in 1874. Authors' Fair Price Estimate: $2,500.

Opposite page
(top) **Marine Chronometer** — Thomas Mercer Ltd., St. Albans, England, No. 19851

Free-sprung detent movement. Helical hairspring, silvered dial with Roman numerals, subsidiary seconds, blued steel hands, and fifty-six-hour up-and-down scale. Mounted in gimbals. Oak case has glazed top. Label on case reads "C.L. Malmsjo, Goteborg." Authors' Fair Price Estimate: $800.

(bottom) **Marine Chronometer** — Thomas Russell & Son, London and Liverpool, No. Aux. 2147 — Circa 1860

Has detent escapement, free-sprung. Silvered dial has black Roman numerals and the Royal Warrant in red, subsidiary seconds and fifty-six-hour up-and-down scale, gold hands mounted in gimbals. Mahogany case is brass-bound and has glazed inner cover. With ratchet key. Authors' Fair Price Estimate: $1,000.

Collector's Gallery II

72 Beginner's Guide to Antique Watches

Swiss Two-Face Watch for the Chinese Market — J. Ullman & Co., Hong Kong and Shanghai — Circa 1900

The front dial is centered with a gilt star on a blue reserve and has black Roman and red Arabic numerals, subsidiary seconds, and openwork gilt hands. The back face is inscribed in Chinese with an outer calendar ring and subsidiary dials as well as a window for moon phases. Blue and white decorations have gilt details. Authors' Fair Price Estimate: $500.

Gilt-Metal Pair Case Repeating Clock Watch — William Dirrick, London, No. 1817 — Circa 1790

Cylinder movement has cock pierced with scrolling foliage and is centered with a ruby end-stone. Dust cap. White enamel dial has Roman numerals and blued steel hands. Strikes and repeats on a bell. Bezel with repeat slide at 8 o'clock. Strike and silence lever between 4 and 5 o'clock. Both cases have pierced borders and are chased with ribbons and flowers. Authors' Fair Price Estimate: $1,950.

Silver Triple-Case Watch for the Turkish Market — Marwick Markham. Perigal, London — Circa 1849

Verge movement with elaborate scrollwork pillars. The cock is pierced with foliate initials above a crescent. The back plate is signed in Turkish. The white enamel dial has Turkish numerals, gold beetle, and poker hands. The first two cases are hallmarked London 1849; the third has silver borders and is covered with tortoiseshell. Authors' Fair Price Estimate: $400.

Quarter Repeating Pair Case Watch for the Turkish Market — Larpent & Jurgensen, Copenhagen — Circa 1740

Verge movement has foliate pierced cock. Quarter repeating on a bell. White enamel dial has Turkish numerals and blued steel hands. A baroque cartouche is at the base and a landscape vignette at the top. The gilt metal outer case is pierced and chased with foliage and has a scalloped rim. Outer case circa 1790. Authors' Fair Price Estimate: $1,900.

(left, top) **Gold Openface Minute Repeating Pendant Watch** — Maker unknown — Late 19th century

Has good lever movement and slide repeat. Engine-turned dial decorated with chased gold flower sprays and a border of running flowers. Movement and dial are Swiss. Case is of heavy gold with shaped sides and chased with formal ornaments centered by the Mexican Eagle. The case is Mexican. Authors' Fair Price Estimate: $2,000.

(left, bottom) **Swiss Gold Hunting Case Quarter Repeating Chronograph** — Audemars Frères, Brassus and Geneva — Circa 1890

Has lever movement and gold cuvette. White enamel dial has a subsidiary dial and pierced gold scrollwork hands. Push repeat. Plain case. Authors' Fair Price Estimate: $1,000.

Opposite page
(top, left) **Swiss Gold Hunting Case Minute Repeating Chronograph** — Maker unknown — Circa 1900

Lever movement and glazed dust cover. Gold cuvette. White enamel dial has subsidiary seconds. The case is chased with three people watching a steeplechase and set with a faceted garnet sun. Authors' Fair Price Estimate: $1,450.

(bottom, left) **Swiss Gold Hunting Case Minute Repeating Watch** — C.J. & A. Perrenaud & Cie., Le Locle — Circa 1890

Lever movement has twenty-seven jewels and slide repeat. Engraved gold cuvette. White enamel dial has blued steel hands and subsidiary seconds. The case is engraved on both sides with birds, foliage, and stars. In center is a gold monogram set with rose diamonds. Authors' Fair Price Estimate: $1,700.

(top, right) **Swiss Gold Hunting Case Minute Repeating Watch** — Montandon, Le Locle — Circa 1890

Lever movement has thirty-five jewels. Gold cuvette is engraved. Chased dial is decorated with gold foliage and has subsidiary dial. Case is engraved on one side with a woman riding side-saddle with a hound alongside, on the other with an Indian amidst flowers, a bird, and a dolphin's head. Authors' Fair Price Estimate: $1,450.

(bottom, right) **Swiss Gold Hunting Case Minute Repeating Chronograph** — Henry Sandoz, Le Locle — Circa 1890

Lever movement and gold cuvette. White enamel dial with subsidiary seconds dial. Slide repeat. Case is engraved with a monogram. Authors' Fair Price Estimate: $1,500.

Collector's Gallery II

Fine Swiss Gold Hunting Case Tourbillon Watch — Signed Capt & Co., Solliat, Switzerland, No. 10871

Three-quarter plate movement, and one-minute tourbillon, with three-arm carriage suspended from steel bridge. The gold cuvette is inscribed "Guggenbuhl-Merian a Bale." Dial is white enamel with black Roman numerals, subsidiary seconds, and blued steel hands. Case is plain. Authors' Fair Price Estimate: $15,000.

Swiss Gold Hunting Case Minute Repeating Chronograph with Perpetual Calendar and Moon Phases — Signed H. Redard & Fils, Geneva, No. 19823 — Circa 1880

Has fine lever movement, thirty-five rubies. Inscribed cuvette. Black Roman numerals on white enamel dial. Subsidiary dials for day of the week, date, month (calibrated for four years), and seconds. Window for moon phases, gold hands, blued steel fly-back hand. Monogrammed plain case. Authors' Fair Price Estimate: $11,000.

Good English Silver Openface Deck Watch — F. Dent, London, No. 23609 — 1856

Gilt full-plate movement with Earnshaw escapement, blued steel helical balance spring, compensated balance. Dial is white enamel with black Roman numerals, blued steel hands, and subsidiary seconds. Back plate and dial have signature. Silver case hallmarked 1856 has gold hinges. Chain and two keys. In mahogany deck case with lid. Authors' Fair Price Estimate: $2,000.

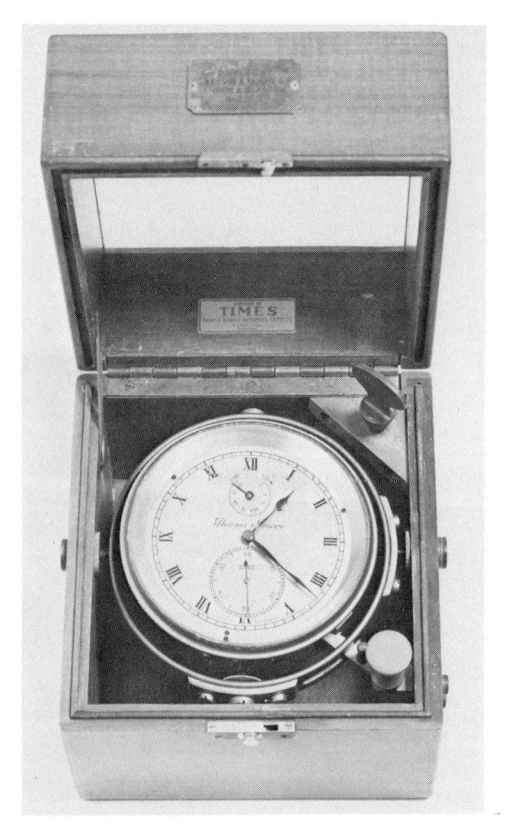

Ship's Chronometer — Thomas Mercer, St. Albans, England, No. 22912

Spring detent escapement, two-arm bi-metallic compensation balance. Silvered dial with subsidiary seconds and fifty-six-hour up-and-down scale. Blued steel hands mounted in gimbals. In wood case with glazed cover. Plate on case inscribed "Supplied by Kelvin & Hughes, London and Glasgow." Authors' Fair Price Estimate: $3,000.

Good Ship's Chronometer — Arnold, Charles Frodsham, 84 Strand, London, No. 2007 — Circa 1850

Spring detent escapement, two-arm bi-metallic compensation balance. Helical steel balance spring. Silvered dial with subsidiary seconds and fifty-six-hour up-and-down scale. Blued steel hands. Spring-mounted dust cap. Brass case in gimbals with lock and ratchet key. Wood case with glazed inner cover applied with ivory roundels. Authors' Fair Price Estimate: $1,500.

Collector's Gallery II

(left) **Deck Watch** — A. Johannsen & Co., 149 Minories, London, No. 8128, Retailed by Lawrence & Mayo, London — Circa 1870

Three-quarter plate, lever movement free-sprung, stem wind. White enamel dial with sweep second hand and blued steel hands. Mahogany deck case has an ivory roundel with number, retailer's name, and the words "Admiralty Pattern Chronometer Watch." Authors' Fair Price Estimate: $400.

(below) **Interesting Silver Box-Form Triple Dial Timer** — Probably Swiss — Mid-19th century

Has form of a rectangular box and is decorated with engine-turned panels. The back has folding belt clip engraved with flowers and foliage. The hinged cover has a small glazed panel to show the hands and champlevé black enamel chapter ring. The interior is mounted with a two-train lever movement. The large white enamel dial has Roman numerals, the smaller dial has Arabic numerals. Folding gold rings for winding and setting. The smaller dial can be set by a lever moving approximately 7½ minutes. The lid is mounted inside with white enamel dial with two hands, calibrated 1 to 10 and 10 to 100. All dials have gold rims. Authors' Fair Price Estimate: $1,200.

(left) **Fine Swiss Gold, Enamel, and Turquoise Pendant Watch and Chatelaine — Maker unknown — Late 19th century**

Formed as three rococo cartouches. Grisaille flowers are enamelled on a black ground surrounded with scrolls decorated by turquoise. The watch has cylinder movement, stem wind, and a cartouche engraved on the back.
Authors' Fair Price Estimate: $3,000.

(right, top and bottom) **Good Swiss Gold and Enamel Ring Watch Set with Jewels — Maker unknown — Late 19th century**

The shape of a beetle with black enamel head and ruby eyes. The wings are enamelled in translucent blue and bordered with graduated old mine diamonds. Wings open to reveal a small watch dial surrounded by radiating black enamel stripes. The back is chased to simulate the insect's body. With diamond set shanks of which one serves to wind the watch.
Authors' Fair Price Estimate: $4,700.

dividend of 150 percent was paid. In 1885 the company became known as the American Waltham Watch Company and twenty years later as the Waltham Watch Company. Its sale of watches, expensive and inexpensive, rose into the tens of millions.

The prize of the line for Waltham was its "Premier Maximus Certificate Watch" which then was the most expensive watch completely made in this country. It was well over twice the price of any others and included the movement and the gold case. Of course, if a buyer wished to decorate it with jewels, he could increase the price astonishingly. The manufacturer insisted the watch was the equal of any other in the world, and certainly its sales brochure showed it had, indeed, a great many most attractive features. The official description follows:

> Twenty-three Diamond, Fine Ruby and Sapphire Jewels; Three Pairs Diamond Caps, Raised Gold Settings; Balance, Pallet and Escape Pivots running on Diamonds; Jeweled Mainwheel Bearings; Red Gold Caps on Pallet, Escape and Fourth Bridges; Accurately Adjusted to Temperature, Isochronism, and Five Positions, and carefully timed in its case at the factory; Compensating Balance, Meantime Screws; Patent Breguet Hairspring Hardened and Tempered in Form; Patent Detachable Balance Staff; Bronze Train; Double Roller Escapement; Sapphire Jewel Pin permanently driven into the roller; Recessed Steel Escape Wheel with Gold Hub; Exposed Red Ruby Pallets; Tempered Steel Safety Barrel; Patent Micrometric Regulator; Steel Parts Highly Finished with Rounded Polished Corners; Patent Winding Indicator showing on the dial the number of hours, up to twenty-four, the watch has run since last winding; Fine Glass Hand-Painted Dial of the most modern and artistic design.

The watch had come a long way since 1500. Just as we have traced the history of Waltham, we could have followed others as well. Certainly by the late 1870s, there were a number of very excellent makers. In fact, there was considerable overcrowding. It was only a matter of time until someone got into low-cost production, and in 1878 D.A. Buck of Worcester, Massachusetts, produced a movement that could be produced cheaply and was not a bad performer. Buck's company was called the Waterbury Watch Co. The watchcase was a barrel holding eight feet of coiled spring round the simplified tourbillon movement. An ingenious variation of the duplex escapement was incorporated in the watch, and the dial was printed on paper, covered with celluloid, and fastened to the plate. The movement turned in the case and carried the minute hand. The movement turned one revolution an hour. There were only fifty-eight parts to the watch, and it sold for $3 with over a half million turned out.

There were problems with the watch which endeared it to buyers then and does so to collectors now. There was that huge length of coiled spring; it took 140 half-turns of the stem to get the watch fully wound. It soon became known as the Waterbury "Long Wind." Jokes were made up about it. "Here, wind my Waterbury for awhile. When you are tired I'll finish winding." The watch was given to couples going on their honeymoon.

What finally killed the poor Long Wind was a lessening of prestige. Many stores started giving away the watch with the purchase of something like a suit. The Waterbury began to be regarded solely as a giveaway.

It was a dozen years later before another watch company again attempted to sell a really cheap watch. The firm was R.H. Ingersoll of Boston, and it came up with a slogan that really worked: "The watch that made the dollar famous."

All this was made possible by the dreams of Dennison and Howard and Henry Pitkin. They saw the need for factory methods and watchmaking machinery. Directly from them came the idea of automatic machinery, such as this machine described in an old publication of the Elgin National Watch Co.:

"The most amazing of these automatics is one which drills, taps and countersinks the holes in the pillar plate, the foundation of the watch. This one machine, which was invented and perfected in the Company's machine shop in about three years' time, automatically performs 85 operations at one setting. It looks like a glass barrel, stood on one end and flooded with jets of oil. It comprises over 14,000 separate parts, three times as many as a modern locomotive, and is made up of 36 smaller machines, arranged in pairs so as to work on both sides of the watch plate at once.

"These 36 units are arranged in pairs at regular intervals, or stations, around a cylindrical frame. An automatic carrier holding 21 blank watch plates stops at the first station. Tools from the twin units engage the plate from above and below, backing off again when their work is done. The carrier moves on to the next station, where other tools are brought into play—till the watch plates have run the gauntlet of all twenty stations and are discharged at the place of beginning.

"In this almost uncanny machine there are 320 gears, and some of them make 7000 revolutions per minute. It is under electric control. If a tool breaks, the machine automatically stops and flashes a light to show which station needs attention. The whole machine is so novel and so complicated in design that skeptics freely predicted it would never work, but time has proved it one of the most efficient machines the Company has yet invented. Behind its veil of oil-spray it performs its manifold operations with super-human precision."

Early watchmakers were troubled turning out specific parts and a very difficult one was the axle or balance staff. Here was how the South Bend Watch Factory handled it years later:

"It is in these turning operations, perhaps, that we find the greatest ingenuity and the greatest interest. For it is here that the most marvelous automatic machines of all with their seemingly human intelligence are to be seen.

"As a typical example of such a machine, examine the workings of one of the automatic marvels which makes balance staffs, the part of the watch that forms the axis for the balance wheel and plays a very important part in correct time-keeping.

"A machine that takes a piece of highest grade carbon steel wire about three feet long, and without human assistance of any kind, fashions from it 150 of the finest balance staffs in the world, each one an exact duplicate of every other, certainly may be said to closely approximate human intelligence in its performance.

"Yet that is exactly what this machine continues to do hour after hour, and the manner of its workings still further impresses the observer with the evidence of an almost uncanny intelligence.

"This machine occupies a space but little larger than an ordinary typewriter and is a marvel of efficiency, probably not exceeded by any other piece of mechanism in existence.

"Ten cutters are mounted on a centrally located axle which can be timed to make almost any sort of cut by means of shifting cams on a large cylinder beneath. This cylinder is provided with a large number of lobes, and by changing the combination between cams and lobes about one thousand different operations may be obtained.

"The balance staffs produced by this machine are made direct from the wire ready for hardening with no other human directions than those given by the men who arranged the combination of cams and lobes. Each separate shoulder on the staffs has both a rough and finished cutter, producing a class of work impossible on the ordinary machine where roughing and finishing is done with the same cutter. There are six shoulders and all of them are made to gauge to the 1/2500th of an inch. The fact that the entire balance staff is completed from the wire while held absolutely rigid in one position insures a truth of alignment that is absolute.

"This remarkable machine, in addition to its skillful performance, displays intelligence in another interesting way. When the end of the wire is reached or if an accident to the piece occurs or the machine itself gets off standard, it automatically stops work and rings a bell summoning a mechanic so that the trouble may be remedied immediately. The pulley which drives the spindle revolves on ball bearings at a speed of 4500 revolutions per minute. Three mechanical principles are used in its operation: compressed air, electric contact, and motor drive. All screws, pinions, jewel settings, etc., are made in much the same manner and by machines very similar to that just described. Batteries of these machines which act with the same marvelous superhuman skill range in long lines down the entire length of several departments of the factory and are continually at work eating up rods of steel and brass and converting them into watch parts of extreme delicacy, minuteness, and exactness."

This, then, is the end product of the work begun so many decades earlier by Howard, and Dennison, who died a poor man, and Henry Pitkin, who died a tragic figure.

America was late on the watchmaking firing line but soon caught up. Today, there are many fine antiques and even common watches of American make that are eagerly sought by collectors.

Some other countries that started late in the making of watches are Japan and, surprising to many laymen, Switzerland. Japan started making watches just one hundred years ago and has become one of the biggest and best of the producers of high precision, jewelled-lever watches. The Japanese previously exhibited the same inventiveness by learning from Western clockmakers and then producing excellent products, not just by imitation but by improvement. When the Seiko Watch-K. Hattori Company went into business, it emphasized precision—"seiko" is the Japanese word for precision. Its first watches are already highly prized collectors' items.

Remarkably, Switzerland also belongs in the late comers listing but for a different reason. The Swiss failed to develop watches with any notable national character. Their watches in the early period tended to be imitative of other countries. Switzerland produced great watchmakers, but they went elsewhere to perform their wonders: Emery and Vulliamy to England and Berthoud, Lepine, and the great Breguet to France. True, the Swiss did have their great enamel painters, such as the Huaud family and Jaquet-Droz in the eighteenth century, but Swiss watchmaking was mostly not aimed at the high-priced market. The Swiss concentrated on clocks and exported inferior watch products for a very long time. In the eighteenth century, England was developing some very fine watches and movements. The cheap movements that some English makers wanted were imported from Switzerland.

The byword in considering a Swiss watch is that the Swiss are capable of making only two types of watches, those that are very, very good and those that can only charitably be referred to as poor to fair. There is no middle ground in Swiss products. Many years ago, one critic stated that the Swiss make the best and worst watches in the world.

Only in the period of mass production of watches did Switzerland really enter the foreground of excellence. Frederic Japy invented many machine tools that allowed the Swiss to mass produce, and it has been only in the last seventy-five years that the Swiss reached the pinnacle of accuracy of performance that has given their work its sparkling reputation.

It becomes another matter when considering the purchase of an old Swiss watch. Is it really a very, very good one or a very, very poor one? Let the buyer beware!

Chapter VII

Tales of Famous Watches

The value of a watch is always enhanced if it has a story to tell or belonged to a famous person. A watch of this type is the skull watch belonging to Mary, Queen of Scots. It was a most interesting watch to begin with, but its value and historical curiosity is further intensified by Mary's fate, which somehow makes her owning a skull watch all the more prophetic and awesome.

It was very large for a skull watch and weighed more than three quarters of a pound. Engraved on its forehead is Death with his scythe. On either side of Death is a palace and a mean cottage. The inscription reads in Latin: "Pale death visits with impartial foot the cottages of the poor and the palaces of kings." Rather a somber thought for a royal lady to have every time she gazes at her watch, but perhaps she was thinking, then, of Elizabeth who had such a well-known fear of death.

The upper right hand side shows Adam and Eve in the Garden of Eden surrounded by animals. The inscription: "By sin they brought eternal misery and destruction on posterity." The other side and back of the watch is given over to the crucifixion of Christ between two thieves.

The skull watch had to be turned upside down, held in one hand, and its lower jaw lifted so that Mary could tell the time. There were more decorations. An engraving, extremely well done, shows the Holy Family in the stable. The illustration of the dial is of Saturn devouring his children.

The movement occupies the brain part of the skull, and the watch is a striking one. The plate is engraved "Moyse, Blois" but gives no date. The watch is undoubtedly from the last half of the sixteenth century. Mary gave the watch to Mary Seton, one of her ladies in waiting, and it was passed down to her descendants, eventually being exhibited at the Royal Scottish Museum at Edinburgh. Somewhere along the line, some fiddling was done with the watch as it has two hands although it was made with only the hour hand.

Queen Victoria had an extremely small watch of gold. It was double cased and pendant wound with a lever escapement. Numbered 5102, it was made for Her Majesty by Breguet in 1838 and had a price of 4250 francs.

Two watches survive from Oliver Cromwell. One, in a silver case, is a small oval watch made by John Midnall in 1625. It is initialed O.C. and shows a small lion holding a tilting spear in its paw. The other, also silver cased, is engraved "Oliver Cromwell" and is dated 1638. It is a large oval alarm watch and has a fishskin outer case. This watch was made in Amsterdam by Bockel. Both watches have only one hand.

Some watches are even more famous than their owners. There is the watch now considered Breguet's greatest work. Just over 2½ inches in diameter, it was ordered in 1783 by an officer in the Marie Antoinette Gardes. It cost 30,000 francs and was not completed for nineteen years, Breguet's watchmaking activities being interrupted by that unpleasantness known as the French Revolution.

All parts were made of gold instead of brass, and the entire movement is visible, covered with rock crystal front and back. The dial is also of crystal. There is an independent second hand, a minute repeater, a perpetual calendar, equation-of-time indicator and a thermometer. It was a self-winder, completed long after Breguet's perpetuelle period. He had given up the device, dissatisfied with the performances of such watches unless he spent a considerable amount of time on them. On this watch, the master did just that, and the watch was a masterpiece of beauty and performance.

Watches can be more than a part of history. They can make history on their own. Such was the case with Lafayette's pilfered watch.

One day early in 1870, a Texan named John R. Ward, on a visit to Louisville, Kentucky, took in a public auction in the hope of finding something worth buying from the property of a Memphis pawnbroker. Rummaging through the goods on display, Ward spotted an old watch with a very worn shagreen cover. It was, Ward told himself, worth looking at. If the cover looked old, perhaps the watch might be an antique of some value. Ward opened the worn cover to find a second case with an allegorical scene. He looked at the back of the inner case and, in the Texan way of putting it, "sucked air." The inscription showed it was a presentation watch given by General George Washington to the Marquis de Lafayette on October 17, 1781!

Ward held his hands as steady as he could and slowly closed the watch and put it back on the display table. He proceeded to look at other items and kept a poker face, an art he'd always felt was important at auction sales. In this case it was vital, not merely to keep the price down but to keep the facts about the watch from being known. If it got out, the bidding would become furious, or the watch would simply be withdrawn.

Ward was also doing some hard thinking about whether the watch was genuine. He had not been able to inspect it very closely because he did not want to attract any attention. However, the more he thought about it, the more he was sure the watch was not spurious. If it had been, it would not have found its way to such an unimportant sale. Clearly, there was no motive here to fool anyone and make a killing. It had to be a very genuine find.

When the auction got underway, Ward was most concerned with the fear that the auctioneer might hold the watch up, study it himself, and perhaps make a last-minute discovery. The fear so panicked Ward that he sat there in cold terror, never once bidding on any of the previous items. When the bidding began on the watch, the auctioneer merely announced the lot number and opened the bidding. Only if the bidding lagged would he stop and try a sales pitch about the watch. Ward quickly made a bid. Another bid followed, and for a moment, Ward thought someone else had made the same discovery that he had. He bid $75.

There were no further bids. Ward had purchased a Lafayette watch for $75! Thus began the strange public saga of the pilfered Lafayette watch, a story that had begun almost ninety years earlier.

On October 19, 1781, as the beaten British troops marched out of Yorktown, a jubilant General Washington gave a number of gifts to officers of France who had aided him in the battle. To Lafayette he presented a watch in a shagreen cover. It was gold and bore the inscription to Lafayette from Washington, dated two days previously when the general had evidently had it inscribed, a reference to the victory over Cornwallis, and the place, Yorktown. The design of the intermediate case depicted, very elaborately, Venus and Mars. The watch was a key wind, and the movement bore the name of an English watchmaker but most likely was Dutch made. Evidently, the general wanted the best for Lafayette and had bought an English one.

Lafayette left Yorktown and returned happily to France, grateful for the gift of the watch which he treasured most highly. Lafayette kept the watch all through his many years of travail during the period of the French Revolution. When he was imprisoned at Olmutz, he was allowed to keep the watch. Even his jailers would not take it from him.

In 1824 Lafayette made a triumphal return to the United States. He was greeted warmly by crowds on every stop of his tour and exhibited the watch to audiences. Often Lafayette was warned to guard the watch more closely, not to exhibit it so freely, and to beware of pickpockets. At Nashville, Tennessee, many festivities were held to honor Lafayette. All living Revolutionary War officers and soldiers were invited by the governor to attend. Some time during Lafayette's stay in Nashville the watch disappeared, most likely stolen.

The news of the watch's theft was not made public. Evidently, Lafayette did not want anything to upset the joyousness of his tour. The Lafayette watch disappeared and stayed lost for almost half a century.

Once John Ward had the watch, he did not keep the Lafayette watch a secret. He attempted to contact the Lafayette family but was unable to do so. Then Ward consigned the watch to be sold. Congress heard about the finding of the watch, and several members insisted it had to be returned to France. Ward turned the watch over to a committee headed by Senator Charles Sumner of Massachusetts, and late in the year 1784, it was forwarded to Elihu B. Washburne in Paris for return to the Lafayette family.

This was not the end of the story of the Lafayette watch since no one knew where it had come from, how Lafayette had lost it, and where it had been for forty-five years.

Then, some anonymous Washingtonian started a private investigation. His story was published in the New York

World, and he was very obviously a man of some importance because he was able to go to the State Department, where it was being kept before being sent to Paris, and was given temporary possession of the watch. The fact that this investigator had this kind of power made it pretty obvious that the story he later told was hardly spurious.

The trail back to the auction was four years old, and before that, there were forty-five years to be explained. The trail went back from the auctioneers to the pawnbroker in Memphis and then to a second pawnbroker in that city. A diligent search through dusty ledgers finally turned up an entry: "June 18, 1868—Miss Matilda Garland, of Jackson, Madison County, deposits a watch..."

It turned out Miss Garland had been around to the pawnbroker herself just three months earlier attempting to redeem the watch. When she was informed it had been sold, she was greatly upset. It turned out that Miss Garland had recently been married to one Paul De Long of Grenada, Mississippi. The De Long trail was traced to Grenada, and the investigator found Mrs. De Long to be a lady of considerable charm and culture. It turned out that during Lafayette's visit to Nashville, the lady's grandfather, Reverend Rufus Garland, rector of St. Mark's Church in Nashville, had acted as one of the fifteen guards of honor. She said that when she found the watch, she had assumed Lafayette must have given it to her grandfather as a remembrance of the event. She was shocked to learn that the watch had been stolen from Lafayette and angrily asserted that her grandfather would never have done such a wicked deed.

It turned out that the Reverend Garland had died in 1847, a date that was to prove most important, leaving only a library of books and a desk to his son, Mrs. De Long's father. Her father had died during the Civil War, and his widow and young daughter had fallen on hard times. Over the years, they sold most of their possessions. Soon all the books were gone, and by 1868 all that remained were two chairs, a bed, and the minister's desk.

Finally it became evident that the desk, too, would have to go. As Mrs. De Long set about cleaning out the drawers of the desk, she accidentally triggered a secret button that revealed a hidden drawer. Inside, they found the watch. It was a godsend. Instead of parting with the desk, they sold the watch for $35.

Happily, shortly thereafter, Mrs. De Long's lot improved, and there was no need for the desk to be sold. Mrs. De Long willingly showed the investigator the desk with the secret drawer. As the investigator studied it, he discovered it was not just a secret drawer but had a false bottom as well.

There were two pieces of paper in this second secret compartment. One was a draft on a London bank for 150 pounds in favor of the Reverend Garland. The other was a long letter concerning the Lafayette watch. Dated December 18, 1846, it read: "This has been a very sad day to me. This forenoon came to me my old friend and comrade, Benjamin Flurnoy of Columbia, in great distress of mind, and asked me to lock the doors and hear him make a disgraceful confession. Then he laid before my astonished eyes the long missing watch of Lafayette, the loss of which caused so much excitement. 'I stole it,' he said; 'I stole it, Rufus.' and hid his face from me. Presently, when I had comforted him, and he grew more calm, he said: 'The doctor tells me I have not long to live; my heart is diseased. I desire you to make restitution for me. Here is all the money needed—take the accursed wedge of Achan from my sight—it has tortured my whole life—restore it to its heirs—without exposing me. I have had misery enough.' He bowed his white head . . . and wept.

" 'How did this happen, Benjamin?' I asked. Said he: 'That night, you remember, we were all upon guard. You and the rest were asleep, but Spatch, Davis, La Crosse and I were on guard for a spell of two hours. We had all been drinking heavily—poor Spatch and Hyacinthe fell asleep on their post, and the devil was in me. I wanted something that belonged to the Marquis. I stole into his room, past old Pouchon, who was snoring. So tired and worn out the old Marquis looked! I opened the trunk, seeking a ribbon, a handkerchief, or the like. The first thing I saw was the watch, and without thinking, I put it in my pocket, raised the window gently, and crept like the thief that I was from the room. As I crossed the threshold I heard the old Marquis call out in his sleep; "Arrêtez vous, Monsieur! Noblesse oblige!" Stung to the quick, I turned back to restore the watch, but just then Pouchon roused, and I escaped. I have never known a happy minute since.'

"My poor friend! I could look in his haggard face, and believe him. I told him, however, that I could not consent to deal with this matter in a clandestine way. There need be no publicity about it, but in communicating with the Marquis' heirs, I must give his name and circumstances. He groaned and begged me to defer the disclosure until after his death. 'It will not be long.' he said pathetically.

"To this I assented, and so he left ... I have drawn this statement up only as a guide for my heirs in case of my death happening before that of Flurnoy's."

This account was printed in the *World* but the investigator's name was never revealed. Neither were any of the other principals identified. All the names in the account as well as the locales of their homes had been changed. The purpose was to learn what had happened to the watch. Clearly that mystery would have been solved a quarter of a century earlier had the Reverend Garland outlived Flurnoy, but he had not. Unfortunately, the watch and the letter of explanation had stayed lost all the many years in the secret drawer of his desk.

This tale of just one watch illustrates the role it played in American history. the purloining of the Lafayette watch had been a blot upon the good name of the nation. That blot was removed only after the watch had been returned to its rightful owner. Oddly, the Lafayette watch ended up being returned to the United States. It remained with the Lafayette family in France for about one hundred years and then in 1948 was put in the possession of an American relative. It passed on by inheritance to another owner in 1963 and not long ago was loaned out to the Smithsonian Institution for exhibit.

Chapter VIII

Should You Invest in Antique Watches?

Do antique watches make a good investment? That is a dirty question to some collectors who accumulate antique watches because of love. Monetary gain is not something to be considered. There is much to be said for this attitude, but it is, of course, silly for a collector to buy watches without some thought of the possibility of selling them at some future time. He should buy some watches he expects will appreciate in value, as well as those he just loves.

We have already remarked about the fabulous jump in value of some railroadmen's pocket watches—from $20 to $150 in just a few years. There is no comparison between a record like that and the dismal performance of the American stock market during the last decade. Of course, there have been many kinds of watches whose prices have stood still for quite a while, and of course, it must be a sobering thought for a watch collector to buy a watch one day and be offered half what he paid for it the next day. However, on quite a few occasions, a watch buyer will find he is offered more for a watch he has just bought by a collector who may have a special need for the particular piece. This can often happen when you bid on a group of watches, and one piece, in particular, is of interest to another collector.

While there is a large dealer markup on antique watches, there is no depreciation that sets in. Let us say you go out and buy a fur coat. The next day the value of that coat has fallen in half. Your chance of finding a private buyer willing to give you what you paid for it is nil. With a dealer you will have a very difficult time because he must think in terms of reselling it and adding his markup. When you buy an antique watch it does not lose any value the next day. The value is still there. You are all the closer to finally turning a profit on it somewhere down the pike.

Overall, the market for antiques has been a slowly rising market for years and years—slow but steady. Naturally, there are the exceptions. Precision watches, especially those by Abraham-Louis Breguet, have been exploding up-

Should You Invest in Antique Watches?

ward. So have really first-class enamels of almost any period, automaton pieces and well preserved early watches. The prices here have gone up quickly, and the experts say this trend will not slow down but continue. Really good antiques, like a good man, are getting harder and harder to find. There is even a sort of "fixing" of the market that keeps prices rising. Museums buy but seldom sell. Millionaires buy but seldom sell. The result is that the supply of good antique watches is shrinking steadily. This does not mean that prices will stop going up despite what the experts say now. Antique collectors' tastes also change. When supplies get too tight in one area, they are likely to shift their interests to another area, one in which the chance to accumulate still exists. Spotting such areas of likely buying is the way to really big profits in antique watches.

If you were attuned to popular thinking a decade or two ago, you might have bought a lot of comic character watches. They have been prime collectibles in recent years. Watches that originally were turned out by such makers as Ingraham, Ingersoll, and the New Haven Watch Company for a mere dollar or two are worth hundreds of times that amount. For instance, a Buck Rogers pocket watch issued in 1935 fetches up to about $400 at retail prices. In the original box the price goes up another $100 or $125. Naturally, this price is for original pieces in mint condition. In average condition, the price could be slashed virtually in half. What about the famous Donald Duck wristwatch of 1935? The price could be as high as $300. Ingersoll put out a new Donald Duck in 1948. The price on this would be at least $150 to $175. Just about the top price in this type of watch is the 1933 Tom Mix Ingersoll pocket watch. It has commanded prices in excess of $600. Generally speaking, pocket watches in this field do better than wristwatches, reflecting greater supplies. The 1934 Popeye pocket watch from New Haven commands prices up to $500 while the 1935 Popeye wristwatch goes for less than half that amount. Similarly, the Lone Ranger 1939 wristwatch by Everbrite sells for somewhat less than $200, but the lapel watch of the same year is worth twice as much.

In addition to cartoon and movie characters, another watch in this category that has become a valuable collectible is the commemorative one. There is the Admiral Byrd watch, named for the explorer of the North Pole, the Graf Zeppelin pocket watch, the 1939 New York World's Fair watch, and so on. More recent watches like those of Richard Nixon, Spiro Agnew, and George Wallace are sure to grow in value with the passage of time. The Wallace watch sells for over $15, and some collectors, perhaps optimistically, expect it to be about $150 in another decade.

Some collectors are buying new versions of comic watches and putting them away with the original packing and receipt. With such authenticity, they can look forward to getting the top prices at any particular time—provided, of course, they have picked a watch that will go up in value.

At the other end of the spectrum—just about as far as one can get from Mickey Mouse—are watches with excellent gold repoussé cases, and continental types of the seventeenth century are starting to grow rapidly in value. Whether they perform as well as a Breguet remains to be seen.

You've decided you want to start collecting antique watches. What do you buy? Again, the main consideration is to buy what you like. You will be keeping it a long time. You should have an interest in it; you should be proud of it; you should be happy if you are "stuck" with it.

The second consideration for a beginner is to "buy cheap." The way to make money in the stock market is to buy low and sell high, but when you go to a stockbroker, he will almost invariably suggest a stock that has already risen quite a bit so you are really buying high in the hope of selling higher. This is fine if you have a lot of money to dabble in stocks. We assume you *don't* have a lot of money to dabble in antique watches. You are looking for watches you can get for $150—or a lot less.

Depending on the locale where you are buying, you can look for certain things. Checking porch sales in New England? Consider that pocket watch. You might luck into a watch worth $150 for just a few dollars. The same holds true at flea markets. Great bargains can turn up in the strangest places. Remember, compared to the average person you are already an expert. Think of the Lafayette watch in the last chapter. It passed through so many hands, including two pawnbrokers and an auctioneer among the so-called "professionals," and was not even spotted as a watch of great

Collector's Gallery III

(above) **Most Unusual Swiss Gold Openface Clock Watch** — E. Gubelin, Lucerne — Circa 1900

Lever movement, dial calibrated 1 to 60 with subsidiary seconds. Single blued steel hand. Chimes once every 5 minutes and twice every 15 minutes. The movement is by Mathey Tissot & Cie., Ponte de Martel. Plain case. Authors' Fair Price Estimate: $800.

(below) **Rare Silver Pair Case Watch** — Signed Ephm. Clark, Philadelphia, No. 436 — Circa 1802

Dial of white enamel with black Arabic numerals and blued steel hands. Verge movement. The cock is decorated with pierced flowers and foliage. A pointing hand is engraved on the foot. Signatures on back plate and dust cap. Cases by E. Maddock, Chester, 1802. Authors' Fair Price Estimate: $1,200.

(above) **Good Swiss Gold Hunting Case Quarter Repeating Chronograph with Calendar and Moon Phases** — Eugene Lecoultre, Geneva — Circa 1890

Good lever movement. Has glazed dust cover, gold cuvette. Dial is of white enamel with black Roman numerals, subsidiary seconds, crescent-shaped register for date with fly-back gold hand and three oval windows for day, month, and moon phases. The case is decorated with borders of chased flowers and leaves on a scrollwork ground. Authors' Fair Price Estimate' $2,800.

Swiss Platinum Openface Minute Repeating Split Second Chronograph — Audemars Piguet, Geneva, No. 17708 — Circa 1930

High grade lever movement. Black Roman numerals on brushed dial. Blued steel hands, subsidiary seconds, and thirty-minute register. The back is brushed and has a champlevé gold monogram. Authors' Fair Price Estimate: $3,000.

Attractive Swiss Gold and Enamel Openface Watch — Patek Philippe & Co., Geneva, No. 147831 — Circa 1909

Lever movement with 20 jewels, inscribed gold cuvette. Black Arabic numerals on white enamel dial. Blued steel hands and subsidiary seconds dial. Back is decorated with monogram on translucent red, dark and light blue enamel. Original case. Authors' Fair Price Estimate: $1,750.

Swiss Gold Hunting Case Repeating Lady's Watch — J. Ullmann & Co., Hong Kong, Shanghai, and Tientsin, No. 40112

Lever movement, slide repeat. Has glazed dust cover, gold cuvette. Dial is of white enamel with black Roman numerals and subsidiary seconds dial. The case is engine-turned. Authors' Fair Price Estimate: $1,250.

Swiss Gold Half Hunting Case Lady's Watch — Patek Philippe & Co., Geneva, No. 55704 — Circa 1880

Lever movement, inscribed gold cuvette. White enamel dial, blue champlevé Roman numerals, subsidiary seconds. Back is monogrammed. Authors' Fair Price Estimate: $600.

Swiss Gold Hunting Case Chronograph — Perrenoud Bros., Le Locle, No. 25123 — Circa 1880

Many-jewelled movement with gold train, gold cuvette. White enamel dial with black Arabic numerals and subsidiary seconds. Chronograph register is calibrated 1 to 300. The case is engine-turned. Authors' Fair Price Estimate: $450.

Swiss Gold Openface Quarter Repeating Montre à Tacte — Patek Philippe & Co., Geneva, No. 19850 — 1861

Lever movement. White enamel dial has Roman numerals 13 to 24, subsidiary seconds between 5 and 6 o'clock. Repeat slide at 10 o'clock. The back is engraved with armorials and supporters above crossed cannons and a row of orders on an engine-turned ground and has a single shaped and engraved hand applied with touchpieces. The arms are those of Gen. Nicolas de Bibkoff to whom the watch was originally sold. Authors' Fair Price Estimate: $7,500.

Collector's Gallery II

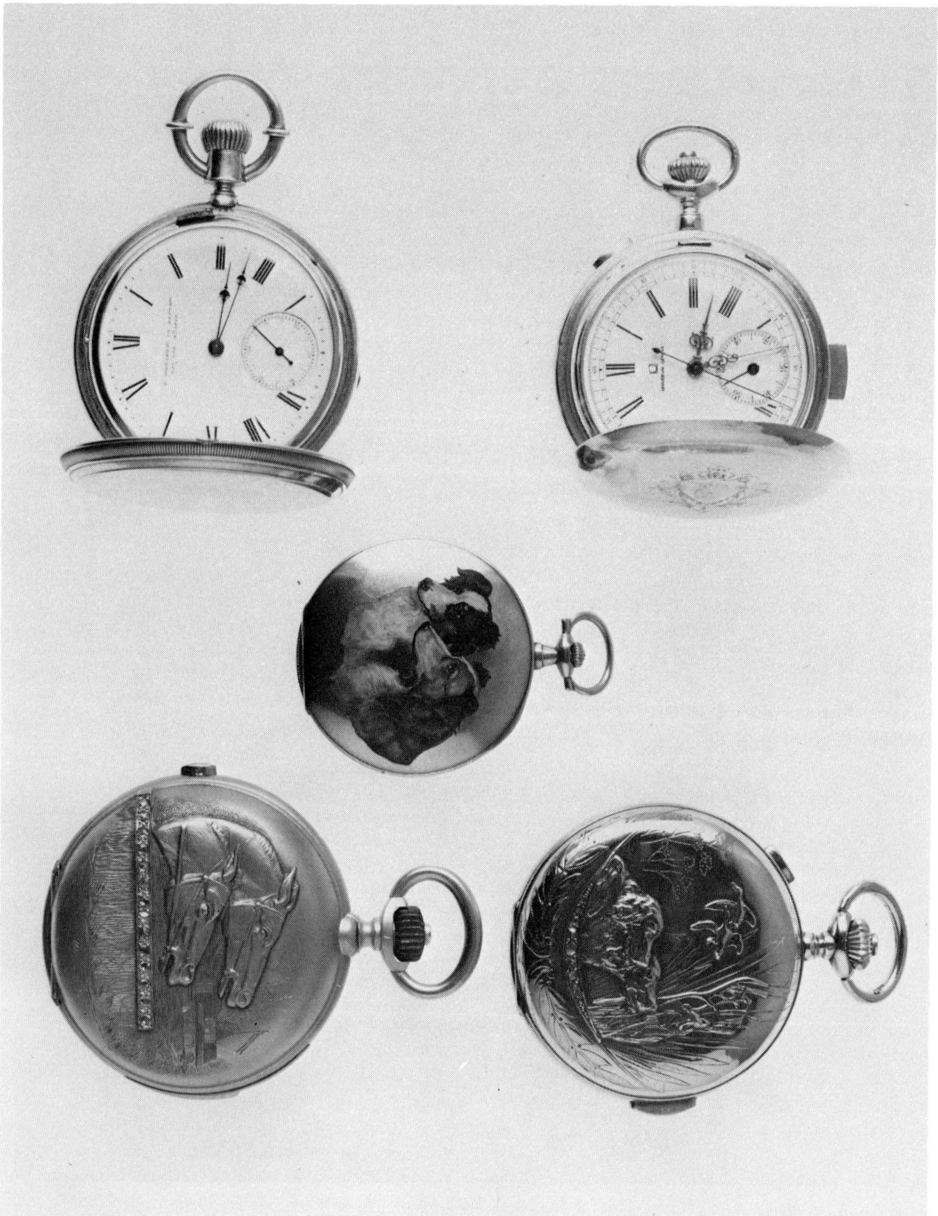

American Gold Hunting Case Watch — E. Howard & Co., Boston, No. 38092 — Circa 1862

Three-quarter plate lever movement with compensation curb. Gold cuvette. White enamel dial has Roman numerals, subsidiary seconds, and slender shaped blued steel hands. Heavy plain case with knurled borders. Authors' Fair Price Estimate: $900.

Swiss Gold Hunting Case Minute Repeating Chronograph — Universal, Geneva — Circa 1900

Has gold cuvette with retailer's name of Casa Escasany, Buenos Aires. Push repeat. White enamel dial has subsidiary seconds, gold scrollwork hands for constant time, blued steel hands for recorded time. Case is engine-turned and engraved with a monogram in a bright-cut shield. Authors' Fair Price Estimate: $1,500.

Swiss Gold Openface Watch — Bonita, Geneva — Circa 1920

Has slim lever movement. Engine-turned dial has subsidiary seconds. Wide bezel has band of translucent orange enamel. The back is enamelled with the heads of two collies. Authors' Fair Price Estimate: $500.

Swiss Gold Hunting Case Minute Repeating Chronograph — Signed Le Fils de R. Picard, Chaux-de-Fonds — Circa 1900

Has twenty-nine jewels, gold cuvette, slide repeat. Dial of white enamel has black Roman numerals I to XII and Arabic numerals 25 to 300. Subsidiary dials at 9 o'clock for seconds and at 3 o'clock for recorded minutes. The matte gold case is decorated with two silver-gilt horse heads above a fence set with rose diamonds. Authors' Fair Price Estimate: $2,100.

Swiss Gold Hunting Case Quarter Repeating Chronograph — Maker unknown — Circa 1900

The movement has glazed dust cover and gold cuvette. Dial of white enamel has pierced gold hands, blued steel chronograph hands, and subsidiary seconds. Push repeat. Front of case has chased scene of two hunting dogs and two flying ducks. A crescent below is set with rose diamonds. Authors' Fair Price Estimate: $1,500.

Swiss Gold and Enamel Hunting Case Lady's Pendant Watch and Diamond Brooch — Movado — Circa 1920

The matte silvered dial is inscribed "Chronomètre à ancre, surete." Gold cuvette also inscribed. The case has stripes of white enamel circled with a ribbon-tied reeded border. A chased patera set with an old mine diamond and bordered by a ring of rose diamonds is mounted in center. The bow-shaped brooch is set with rose diamonds. Authors' Fair Price Estimate: $750.

Swiss Gold and Enamel Hunting Case Lady's Watch — Maker unknown — Circa 1880

Lever movement. Gold cuvette has enamelled scene of putti and lamb surrounded by flowers. Dial of white enamel has subsidiary seconds. The case is decorated with champlevé black enamel. Sides are shaped and center is engraved with urn held by grotesque animal figures. Authors' Fair Price Estimate: $300.

Swiss Gold and Pearl Lady's Pendant Watch and Brooch — L. Bachmann, Geneva — Circa 1900

Has cylinder movement. White dial has red Arabic numerals, gold scrollwork hands. The back is of pave with pearls and red pastes in flower design. The brooch is shaped like a swallow, of pavé set with pearls and with ruby eyes, suspended from a gold chain. Authors' Fair Price Estimate: $550.

Swiss Gold and Enamel Hunting Case Lady's Watch — Deoeilh & Cie., Geneva — 1860

With key-wind cylinder movement and gold cuvette. Engine-turned silver dial is decorated with gold foliage. The front has a portrait of a girl in a pink dress with flowers in her hair painted in enamel. The portrait is set with three stones within a black enamel strapwork border. The back is enamelled in blue with a similar border. Authors' Fair Price Estimate: $500.

Swiss Gold and Diamond Hunting Case Lady's Pendant Watch and Brooch — Retailed by Tiffany & Co., New York — Circa 1910

Lever movement. Gold cuvette. White enamel dial has subsidiary seconds. Plain case has a large diamond centered in front. Back is engraved with monogram. Has a rope-twist brooch. Authors' Fair Price Estimate: $450.

Lady's Onyx, Gold, and Diamond Pendant Watch and Brooch — Maker unknown — Circa 1880

Cartouche-shaped watch is carved of onyx with bevelled borders. The white enamel dial is circled with rose diamonds. The oval cylinder movement has hinged glazed cover. Watch is suspended by gold chains from a curved bar brooch. Authors' Fair Price Estimate: $650.

Swiss Gold and Diamond Hunting Case Lady's Watch — Lagrange — Circa 1900

Lever movement. Gold cuvette. White enamel dial has subsidiary seconds. Case is of matte gold chased with a horse and jockey jumping through a horseshoe, set with rose diamonds backed by a spray of laurel. Authors' Fair Price Estimate: $350.

Collector's Gallery II

104   Beginner's Guide to Antique Watches

(left, top) **Gold and Enamel Openface Watch for the Turkish Market** — Signed Leroy et Fils, Horlogers du Roi, à Paris — Circa 1830

Has cylinder movement and engine-turned cuvette. Dial of white enamel has Turkish numerals and signature. Hands are of blued steel. The case is scalloped and enamelled with a ship at sea bordered with orange and white enamel. Panels of pink and translucent green enamel are decorated with multi-colored and grisaille bouquets. The bezel, pendant, and bow have matching decoration. The case is of Swiss origin. Authors' Fair Price Estimate: $1,250.

(left, bottom) **Swiss Silver-Gilt and Enamel Minute Repeating Hunting Case Watch** — Schwab Frères & Co., Chaux-de-Fonds, Geneva — Late 19th century

Has glazed dust cover. Slide repeat. White enamel dial has subsidiary seconds and openwork hands. Both sides are enamelled with portraits of girls on a blue ground framed with pointed borders and circled with pearls. Authors' Fair Price Estimate: $2,000.

Collector's Gallery II

Opposite page

(right, top) **Swiss Gold and Enamel Openface Watch for the Turkish Market** — Maker unknown — Circa 1825

Has cylinder movement. The gold cuvette is enamelled in blue with the details of the movement and the name Breguet à Paris. The white enamel dial has gold openwork hands and Turkish numerals. The back is enamelled with a spray of flowers on a primrose ground. Surrounding geometric borders are enamelled with scrolls and flowers on pink and blue grounds. Bezel, pendant, and bow are decorated to match. Authors' Fair Price Estimate: $550.

(right, center) **Silver-Gilt and Enamel Lady's Openface Watch for the Oriental Market** — Maker unknown — Circa 1830

The detached lever movement is elaborately chased with scrolling foliage. White enamel dial has Roman numerals and sweep second hand. The back is enamelled with the portrait of a young girl on translucent orange enamel over an engine-turned ground. The borders, pendant, and bow are set with pearls. Authors' Fair Price Estimate: $500.

(right, bottom) **Viennese Silver-Gilt and Enamel Oval Watch** — Maker unknown — Late 19th century

Case is enamelled on the back with Venus and cupid. The sides show landscape vignettes with classical ruins on a gilt ground. The interior is enamelled with a cupid riding a dolphin. The dial is decorated with champlevé translucent and opaque enamels and with Roman numerals. The verge movement has the signature Breguet à Paris. The bow is of enamelled trefoil. Authors' Fair Price Estimate: $1,200.

(right, top) **Swiss Silver-Gilt and Enamel Openface Watch for the Oriental Market** — Maker unknown — Mid-19th century

Cylinder movement is elaborately chased and has glazed dust cover. White enamel dial has black Roman numerals and subsidiary seconds. The back is enamelled with an abundant spray of flowers on a pale grey ground and circled with pearls. Authors' Fair Price Estimate: $1,200.

(right, bottom) **Viennese Silver-Gilt and Enamel Pear-Shaped Watch** — Maker unknown — Late 19th century

Body is enamelled with courtly figures in a landscape. The interior also has a landscape painted in enamel. The movement has a white enamel dial and bears the signature of Breguet à Paris. Hands are missing. Authors' Fair Price Estimate: $800.

Swiss Gold Hunting Case Lady's Watch — Montandon Frères, Geneva — Circa 1880

Lever movement and gold cuvette. Engine-turned silver dial is decorated with chased gold flowers and foliage and has subsidiary seconds. Shell-shaped case is engraved with formal foliage. Authors' Fair Price Estimate: $300.

Swiss Silver Skull Watch "Hamlet" Model — Maker unknown — Circa 1900

The skull opens to reveal a white enamel dial with subsidiary seconds. The cranium is engraved "Ultima Forsam." Authors' Fair Price Estimate: $400.

Swiss Gold Lady's Hunting Case Pendant Watch — Montandon, Le Locle — Circa 1870

Cylinder movement. Engine-turned dial adorned with two-color gold chased foliage. The shaped case is engraved with sprays of flowers enclosed by anthemia and feather scrolls. Authors' Fair Price Estimate: $250.

Swiss Gold and Enamel Lady's Openface Watch — Maker unknown — Circa 1900

Has cylinder movement. The back is enamelled with a cupid on a crescent man-in-the-moon and has two rose diamond stars. Authors' Fair Price Estimate: $150.

Swiss Gold and Diamond Lady's Hunting Case Watch — Maker unknown — Circa 1875

Has cylinder movement. Engine-turned dial has chased gold decor. Front of case is enamelled with a blue and red butterfly set with rose diamonds. Back of case has small butterfly painted in enamel sitting on a flowering branch. Authors' Fair Price Estimate: $200.

Swiss Gold and Enamel Lady's Hunting Case Watch — Maker unknown — Circa 1860

Has cylinder movement. White enamel dial. Both back and front are set with rose diamonds on a black enamel ground. Borders are of engraved scrolls. Authors' Fair Price Estimate: $300.

Swiss Gold and Enamel Lady's Hunting Case Pendant Watch and Brooch — Bernardi, Geneva — Circa 1870

Lever movement has seventeen jewels. Engine-turned dial has chased gold foliage. The case is chased with formal foliage and decorated with black enamel. The front is set with rose diamonds. Bow-shaped brooch is decorated with black enamel and set with rose diamonds. Authors' Fair Price Estimate: $750.

Swiss Gold and Enamel Lady's Hunting Case Watch — Louis Brandt, Geneva — Circa 1850

Has

Has cylinder movement. White enamel dial. Case is chased and enamelled on both sides with blue foliage and white berries on a leaf-chased background. Has a gold ratchet key. Authors' Fair Price Estimate: $300.

Collector's Gallery II

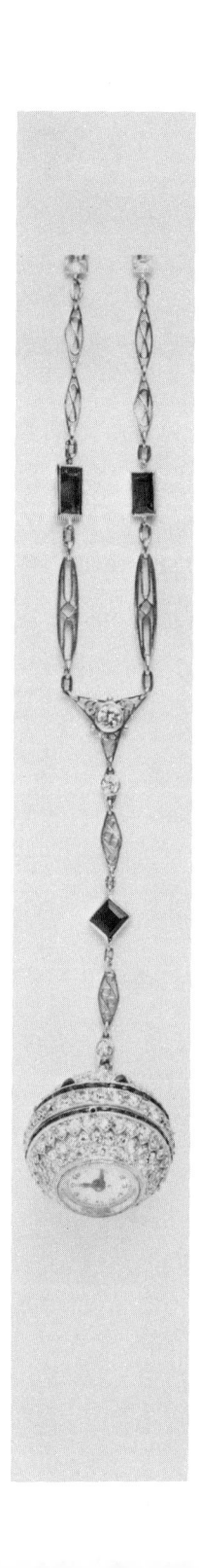

(left) **Diamond and Sapphire Ball Watch with Matching Chain** — Circa 1920

The watch pavé with diamonds and with sapphire borders. The platinum chain set with alternating emerald-cut diamonds and sapphires. Authors' Fair Price Estimate: $1,500.

Opposite page
(top, left) **Swiss Gold, Enamel, and Diamond Drop-Shaped Pendant Watch** — Circa 1900

White enamel dial with blue and red Arabic numerals, decorated with translucent pink enamel, bordered by red and white enamel lines. Mounted in a calyx of stiff leaves set with rose diamonds. Matching suspension loop. Authors' Fair Price Estimate: $700.

(bottom, left) **Gold, Enamel, and Diamond Lapel Watch and Brooch** — Circa 1920

The octagonal watch is decorated with black enamel within white line borders, mounted with a diamond vase of flowers. It is suspended from a bar brooch set with diamonds, with black enamel lozenge-shaped center. The suspension loop is also set with diamonds. Authors' Fair Price Estimate: $700.

(center) **Swiss White Gold, Diamond, and Pearl Lapel Watch and Brooch** — Circa 1900

Cylinder movement. The back pavé with pearls and rose diamonds. The bow knot brooch formed of pearls centered by an openwork square arrangement of diamonds with large central diamond. Authors' Fair Price Estimate: $2,000.

(right) **Platinum Pendant Watch and Chain** — Circa 1910

The octagonal watch chased with scrolled strapwork set with diamonds and an octagonal border of baguette-cut onyx. The movement by the Waltham Watch Co. is suspended from a platinum chain set with pearls alternating with onyx beads. Authors' Fair Price Estimate: $1,200.

Collector's Gallery II

110 Beginner's Guide to Antique Watches

(left) **Art Deco Platinum and Onyx Lapel Watch and Brooch Set with Diamonds and Rubies** — Maker unknown — Circa 1930

The marquise-shaped watch has onyx back and is centered with a diamond and has a diamond border. The brooch is an onyx ring flanked with two cabochon rubies and surrounded with diamonds in arrow-shaped mounts. The shaped suspension-piece is set with large and small diamonds. Authors' Fair Price Estimate: $2,500.

(second from left) **White Gold, Diamond, and Onyx Pendant Watch and Brooch** — Maker unknown — Circa 1930

Octagon-shaped watch is mounted with an onyx panel bordered by diamonds suspended by diamond-set chains from a matching patera and bar pin. The dial is inscribed "Tusten, New York." Case is fitted. Authors' Fair Price Estimate: $2,700.

(second from right) **French Art Deco Platinum, Onyx, and Diamond Lapel Watch and Brooch** — Van Cleef & Arpels, Paris — Circa 1920

The tulip-shaped watch has onyx back centered and bordered with diamonds and with a diamond set cresting. The sides are engraved with key-pattern. The brooch is vertical and decorated in a chequer pattern of diamonds and onyx. Authors' Fair Price Estimate: $1,250.

(right) **Art Deco Platinum, Diamond, and Jade Lapel Watch and Brooch** — Maker unknown — Circa 1930

The watch is oval-shaped and the back decorated with alternating stripes of diamonds and baguette jades. The elongated brooch is decorated with flower heads of diamonds with sapphire centers. The crown is set with a trefoil of three pear-shaped jade cabochons with a crest of diamonds. The suspension piece is mounted with a single large emerald-cut diamond. Authors' Fair Price Estimate: $3,200.

(left) **Fine Art Nouveau Gold Openface Minute Repeating Watch with Perpetual Calendar and Moon Phases** — Signed B. Poitevin, 22 Rue Vivienne, Paris, No. 48856 — Circa 1903

Lever movement of high quality. Gold cuvette is inscribed, dial has black Arabic numerals, subsidiary dials for the day of the week, month (calibrated for four years), and seconds. Window for moon phases. The repoussé case has chased sprays of ivy and initials on a matted ground. Authors' Fair Price Estimate: $12,000.

(below, left) **Swiss White Gold and Diamond Dress Watch with Gold Movement** — Gruen, 50th Anniversary Watch, No. 223

Twenty-one jewels and two diamonds give this watch extra precision; the bridges are chased with scrolling foliage. Brushed dial is set with round and baguette-cut diamonds and features raised numerals, subsidiary seconds. The case is pentagonal and has borders of chased leaves. Authors' Fair Price Estimate: $2,000.

(below, right) **Fine Swiss Gold Openface Minute Repeating Split Second Chronograph with Perpetual Calendar and Moon Phases** — Signed Bigelow, Kennard & Co., Boston, Mass., No. 5114 — Circa 1898

Lever movement, gold cuvette. Black Arabic numerals on white enamel dial. Subsidiary dials for the day of the week, date, month, and seconds with a window for moon phases. Monogrammed back. Authors' Fair Price Estimate: $10,000.

Should You Invest in Antique Watches?

value. There are places you can buy old watches the backs of which no one has opened. There are antique dealers with watches they don't even know how to open!

There are bargains on antique watches everywhere, and the fun is hunting them out. Of course, you will patronize watch dealers and antique shops. There is a lot you can buy within the limit of $150. For half the sum, you can get small, enamelled gold watches. These would be late eighteenth and early nineteenth century pieces. What you are looking for is something in good condition. Pass up scratched enamel and rubbed engravings. Check the hinges and catches. most experts feel that engraved, gold-cased watches of the mid-Victorian period will go up in value, especially if there is a good pictorial decoration. In this period, the least promising growth seems to be in silver-cased watches and engravings with regular floral scenes. The best rule of thumb, in these cases, is to look for one with a name in it. A name is a name is a name and is far better than no name. There is another "kicker" behind this. Watches of the post-1825 period have not really been subject to historical documentation. When this is done, the name on a watch may well take on more meaning than it has now. It could be a real find.

Another good area to explore is the late eighteenth and early nineteenth century base metal, enamelled watches. However, you should like them, yourself, for their own sake. Some people feel they are too garish and won't buy them, but there are always buyers for the better examples of the group.

One type of watch that has been doing very well in the last few years has been eighteenth century silver-cased watches with painted enamel dials. They have been the rage, and prices have gone up sharply, starting in the previous decade. Certain scenic displays have tended to add to the value. Of these, the railroad train seems to be doing best of all.

Probably the best argument of all can be used in favor of any gold watch. The value of gold has risen sharply from the old price of $35 an ounce. Like OPEC oil it has more than quadrupled. There are very few economists around who expect to see the price of gold go through the floor. On the other hand, there are plenty of "gold bugs" around who foresee gold rising to $300 an ounce, $500 an ounce, or even more, not too far in the future. If they are right, a gold antique watch has not one but two ways to grow. The gold watch could have an even better future ahead of it than a first-class enamelled case.

Watches make the best buy, but it is possible to specialize in collecting just cases or parts of watches, such as fobs, watch cocks, keys, watch paper, stands, tools, alarm and repeating mechanisms. For a time, watch cocks were extremely popular, but such trends can be short-lived. The appeal of the complete watch remains the safest bet for a beginner. When you are much more expert and have a genuine desire to do so, you can start thinking about collecting parts.

Whatever you buy or collect, caution should always be the byword. Antique watches are a ripe field for fakes. This is not the time or place to go into any detailed rules on how to spot a fake antique watch. A few pat rules will not provide all the answers and can lull a new collector into a false sense of security. The best defense is to buy from regular sources, those you have learned to trust. Your garageman is less likely to cheat you if he knows you are a regular customer, one who will go on buying his gas and oil. So too with watch dealers. The satisfied customer, they know, will come back while the suspicious one won't.

Probably the most "faked" area of watches is the period from 1550 to 1650, happily an era the beginner is not likely to and really should not enter. But it is a good area to study because one starts to categorize each area by style, by technology, and so on. Remember that the art of fakery in antique watches is an old one. A buyer today may be fooled by a shady character who did his foul deed one hundred and fifty years ago. Learn to recognize what shape a watch of a certain period is likely to be in. If a watch is in perfect condition in an era when most watches are not, enthusiasm should be contained. Question why this watch is in so much better shape. Was it worn by a little old lady who wound it only on Sundays? The fact remains, the further you go back, the less likely it is that a watch will be in perfect condition, so the more suspect such a piece should be.

Some fakes have been so good that museums have held special exhibitions for them, and they have become prized collectors' items. but, here come the fakers again! If you want a wonderful fake, great! But beware, when fakes become valuable, it often can pay for a faker to doctor up a genuine item to *appear* to be a fake! In the fakery business, there are twists within twists within twists.

But that again is the fun of it all. Playing Sherlock Holmes with watches is an invigorating exercise. One leading authority, wishing not to be identified, says he has such a feeling of exhilaration when he finds a fake that he has to curb his enthusiasm and not jump to the desired conclusion too soon. Some dealers and collectors go out of their way to call watches fakes when they are genuine. Of course, this is a time-honored technique to force the price down so they can buy the item for a song. But often there are other mean motivations. They may not want the watch themselves, but because of jealousy or for competitive business reasons, they may cry fake. A dealer may be trying to sow suspicion in the buyer's mind about the party who sold the watch originally.

It is too bad that the field has not reached the point yet that impartial experts can be found who can say yes or no with honest authority in every possible case. It is you who must be the judge and the detective. It is you who, in time, will be able to pick up an old watch, look at it, and announce it is genuine. "This watch has a balance spring which is not original. See these holes. That shows where the stackfreed was removed. It may not have appeared so at first, but this is a German watch. Over-restored, granted, but genuine."

On the other hand, you would be suspicious of another watch that looks too good for its age. "Why haven't these sharp edges and high points of the design lost their gilding? If this movement is genuine, why aren't there signs of wear? The holes should have been rebushed. There could be some later wheels and pinions. Peculiar. I want to think more about this one. I've got to say this one could be—probably is—a fake. When in doubt, I don't buy."

When you get really good at your avocation, you will learn that most fakers weren't all that good. If they were, they could have become watchmakers instead. Few are thorough students of the field. The iron work may be too coarse and heavy, and where the ornamentation should be Renaissance, it may be Gothic, by mistake. Where catches should be used, there are pins. Where there are screws there should have been pins. If you do your homework, you will know that with brass movements, steel was still used for springs and arbors. You will become expert on these and numerous other little errors that fakers make.

All this is for "defensive buying." The buyer who is not fooled and does not overpay still has money to spend when the watch that he really must have comes along. You do that by knowing the periods, the makers, and their styles. Does this particular watch fit the style of the supposed maker? How much repairing and restoring has been done on the watch? If you are willing to take it in that condition, is the next person just as likely? Does the watch need work, and how much will that add to the cost? Some watch buyers have been shocked at what the final cost of putting a watch in good shape came to. If two watches of the same general quality sell for a wide difference in price, you will learn that the difference generally works out to the cost of getting it in working order. If the disparity is too great or too little, one or the other of the watches is overpriced.

You are investing in watches whether or not you ever plan to sell those you buy. If you buy six watches with "X" number of dollars, and the next person buys six watches of similar quality for the same money and still has enough money to buy four more watches, he is the one doing the real investing. He will see the value of his collection grow and grow, and he will be the one who savors all the joys of collecting antique watches.

You should, too. You can be buying enjoyment and beauty and a sense of history and value. There are few bargains in life to match that! Happy hunting!

Appendix A

Important Dates in the History of Watches

There is no way to compile a complete and accurate chronology of events in the history of watches. Records are often poor and many times have to be approximated and deduced. No one should read this list with the idea that it is gospel. Sometimes an important discovery or invention is made and then ignored for years or even decades. Styles and techniques were at odds with each other in different countries, in different cities, in fact within cities from one watchmaker to another. One watchmaker's work would often conflict with something he'd done previously. However, it is important to have an awareness of the broad sweep of events in the world of watches and this is an attempt.

Pre-1500	Watches started appearing in Europe.
1500	Peter Henlein developed his mainspring.
1510	Peter Henlein produced his first watch.
c 1510	The stackfreed came into use for the first time to control the tension on the mainspring.
1525	Jacob Zech introduced the fusee.
1560	Watches began to be made in different shapes such as oval or egg shaped.
1580	Watches in the shape of crosses, fruits, flowers, and insects became popular and were known as toy watches.
1587	Charles Cusin started the watchmaking trade in Geneva, Switzerland.
1600	The pocket watch evolved from the portable watch.
c 1600	Watchmaking began in London.
1610	Dials were being protected with watch glasses for the first time.
1610	Watch cases were first decorated with enamel.
1630	Limoges produced the first watches painted with enamel.
1632	Varicolored enamel painting was the most desired decoration of watch cases.
1635	Paul Viet, of France, introduced enamel dials.
1640	Tortoiseshell, horn, and shagreen were first used to make outer watch cases.
c 1650	The first Puritan watches appeared.
c 1650	Round watch cocks were first used.
c 1650	The tulip pillar was applied in watch mechanisms.
1658	Robert Hooke invented the straight balance spring for watches.
1660	The minute hand was introduced.
c 1670	Watch fusees were made of chain rather than gut.
1674	Abbe de Hautefeuille and Huygens invented the curved balance spring.
c 1675	The first watch pocket appeared on a waistcoat.

c 1675	First pair watch cases were made.
1680	Second hands were added.
1687	First repeating watch made by Barlow and Quare.
1694	Nicholas Facio first used jewels in watches.
1695	Thomas Tompion invented the cylinder escapement.
c 1700	Experimentation with unusual watch dials began.
c 1700	The so-called pendulum watch sold by second-rank makers.
c 1700	Egyptian pillars first used in watch mechanisms.
1725-1750	Repoussé watch cases were the fashion.
c 1750	Most desirable watch dials were of white enamel.
1770	Francis Guerint first used engine turning for decorating watch cases.
1770	The lever escapement came into use.
1776	Lepine first produced very thin watches.
1780	The second hand was now widely in use.
1780	The first self-winding watch was introduced.
1790-1820	Watches with moving figures and musical watches were invented.
1798	L. Perron produced the pin lever watch escapement.
1800	Pearls began to be used for decorating watches.
c 1800	The pair case was replaced by the single watch case.
c 1800	Guillochet watch cases appeared.
1801	First tourbillon watch was made.
1820	First watch with keyless winding made.
1842	Watches could be set by hand with a button for the first time.
1850	Plans laid for mass production of watches in America.
1853	First factory-made watches were sold.
1854	Watch factory was established at Waltham.
c 1865	The first railway watch, the Roscopf, introduced.
c 1865	Pocket chronometers the vogue.
1880-1896	Waltham watches produced in huge numbers in America, including later the "Premier Maximus Certificate Watch," selling for $750.
1900	Wrist watches captured the public's eye.
1927	Buster Brown pocket watch appeared.
1928	The Explorer watch, honoring Admiral Byrd, issued by Ingraham.
1933	Mickey Mouse pocket and wrist watches joined the comic character watch parade.
1957	Hamilton Watch Co. made the first electric wrist watch.
1959	Bulova issued the Accutron tuning fork wrist watch.
1970	Atomic wrist watch developed by McDonald Douglas.

Appendix B
Prominent Watchmakers Around the World

Following are some names of prominent watchmakers from around the world. Any collector must always have such a list to refer to. It is invaluable in the identification and dating of watches. Some names on the list may be clockmakers to a greater extent than watchmakers while others may either be exclusively watchmakers by profession or at least by inclination. The dates given with each name may be the dates the individual lived, when he was active making watches, a specific date found on one of his watches, or the date of his death. It is difficult, if not impossible, to be any more specific.

Sometimes the first name is unknown or only initialed. Identification of watchmakers is often a form of detective work. Books for more advanced collectors contain more names, many quite obscure. Eventually, as you become more involved in old watches, you will need the truly comprehensive lists. One most indispensable reference book is G.H. Baillie's *Watchmakers and Clockmakers of the World* which contains the names of over 35,000 craftsmen from all over the world up until about 1825. There is no absolutely complete single list for later watchmakers. You will need to build a reference library and to search each book when you come across a name needing identification. Of course, this is hardly work but part of the fun of watch collecting.

Abraham, Ebenezer. Olney. Watch, 1773.
Achard, G. Geneva, Switzerland. Watch, 1810.
Ackers, W. St. Andrew's. Pair-case watch, about 1705.
Adam, Melchior. Paris. Octagonal watch, late 16th century.
Adams, William. Boston. First quarter 19th century.
Adamson, John. London. Gold minute watch, 1686.
Ageron, François. Paris. Gold watches, mid-18th century.
Aicken, George. Cork. Watch, 1780.
Akced, J. London. Watch, 1795.
Alexander, Isaac. Nottingham. Watch, about 1760-70.
Amant. Paris. Inventor of the pin wheel escapement, 1749.
Anderson, Alex. London. Watch, 1770, possibly same Alex. Anderson in Liverpool with watch in 1786.
Anderson, J. London. Watch, 1775.
Anderton, J. London. Repeating watch, about 1750.
Angoille, Jean. Paris. 1690-1712.
Anjou, Jean Gustave. Stockholm. 1771-90.
Anthony, William. London. Important maker of fine watches until 1844.
Antram, Joseph. London. Important clock- and watchmaker from about 1700 to about 1720. Watch- and clockmaker to His Majesty.
Arlaud, Henry. London. Very fine calendar watches, 1630.
Arnold, John. London. 1736-1799. Invented helical balance spring for chronometers. Made repeating watch in ring for George III, 1764.
Aspinwall, Samuel. Clock-watch about 1660.
Atherton, Nathan. Philadelphia. Watches about 1825.
Atkinson, Mary. Baltimore. Watches, 1802-07.
Attemstetter, David. Augsburg. Important enameller, died 1617.
Augier, Hehan. Paris. Very large watches, 1650.
Avice, —. Reims. Watches, 1723.
Azemard, Jacques. Geneva. Watches, 1770-90.
Baccuet, —. Enamelled watch, about 1690.
Backhouse, John. Lancaster. Watch, 1726.
Bagnall, Benjamin. Philadelphia. Watches, 1749-53.
Bailey, John. Boston. Watches, 1803-15.
Bailey, William. Philadelphia. 1820.
Baillon, Jean Baptiste. Paris. 18th century watches, described as the richest watchmaker in Europe.

Bainbridge, George. Dublin. Watches, 1766-95.
Baker, Benjamin H. Philadelphia. 1824.
Baker, Richard. London. Watches, repeating, pendulum, 1685.
Banger, Edward. London. 1695-1713.
Barlow, Edward. London. Invented the rack striking work, and was associated with Thomas Tompion. Died 1716.
Barnes, Robert. Liverpool and Birmingham, 1754-78.
Barnhill, Robert. Philadelphia. 1777.
Baronneau, Louys. Paris. Very fine watches, 1640-64.
Barrow, Nathaniel. London. Complicated watch, second half of 17th century.
Barry, Standisk. Baltimore. Watches, 1784-1804.
Barton, T & J. Manchester. 1770.
Barton, William. London. 1780.
Basset, John F. Philadelphia. 1798.
Bath, Thomas. London. 1749-84.
Baudet. Paris. Gold enamel watches, early 19th century.
Bauer, Carl. Amsterdam. Cruciform watches, 1650.
Bayes, John. London. Made watches for Charles I, 1647.
Beaufort, Henri. Paris. Watch with decimal time, 1796.
Bedford, Isaac. Dublin. Watches, 1795-1824.
Beitelrock, Johann. Augsburg. About 1736-57.
Bell, Benjamin. London. Maker of large verge watch weighing half a pound, last half of 17th century.
Bell, William. Philadelphia. 1805.
Benedict, S.W. New York. Until 1835.
Bergeau, or *Bergeo, Peter.* London. 1715-70.
Berrollas, Joseph A. London. Brilliant watchmaker, patented a repeater in 1808, a warning watch in 1810, an alarm watch in 1827.
Berthoud, Ferdinand. Paris. Born in Switzerland, but emigrated to France where he became a leading watchmaker, author of many works on subject.
Betts, Samuel. London. Mid-17th century.

Bird, Richard. London. Watch chain maker, 1794.
Bittleston, John. London. Made very unusual watches, 1765-94.
Bock, Johann. Frankfurt. Various oval calendar watches, 1620-40.
Bockels, —. Amsterdam. Made watch for Oliver Cromwell, 1640.
Boncher, A. London. Musical watchmaker, 1835.
Bond, William. Boston. First U.S. chronometer, 1812.
Booth, Ben. London. 1780.
Bordier, A. Geneva. Watches in enamelled cases, octagonal cases, about 1800.
Bouquet, David. London. 1630s to 1665.
Bovet, —. Brothers made watches for China, 19th century.
Brandt, Charles. London. Famous musical watchmaker, 1815-35.
Breguet, Abraham-Louis. French watchmaker, the best of all. Born 1747, died 1823.
Buschman, David. Augsburg. Excellent watchmaker but watches almost a century apart credited to him. Some aren't his.
Cabrier, Charles. London. 1729-59.
Caron, Peter Auguste. Made watch for the king, another for Madame de Pompadour. Also skilled musician, wrote "Barber of Seville" under the name of Beaumarchais. Died 1799.
Carter, Jacob. Philadelphia. 1806.
Chamberlain, Thomas. London. Calendar and striking watches, about 1630.
Chauvell, James D. London. Clock-watches and repeaters, early 18th century.
Cheson, Salomon. Blois. Made timepiece for Marie de Medicis. Died about 1634.
Cheson, Solomon. Blois. Made watch without hands, instead having an escutcheon engraved on plate that revolved inside hour circle. 1673.
Clark, Ephraim. Philadelphia. 1780-1813.
Clay, Charles. London and Yorkshire. Died 1740.
Cole, James. London. Called "The English Breguet." Died 1880.
Colley, Richard. London. Died 1736.

Combret, Pierre. Lyons. 1613.
Comtesse, Louis. Watch case maker. 1810.
Dakin, James. Boston. 1796.
DeBaufre, Peter. London. Watchmaker for Sir Isaac Newton and invented a "club-footed" verge escapement.
Dennison, Aaron L. Associated with Edward Howard in first real watch factory in U.S.
De St. Leu, Daniel. London. Watchmaker to George III. Second half of 18th century.
Dubie, J. Paris. Court goldsmith, master of fine enamelled watch cases. Mid-17th century.
Duchesne, Francois Houet. One of the leading Paris watchmakers. 1725-40.
Edmonds, James. Charleston. 1745.
Elvin, William. Baltimore. Beginning of 19th century.
Emery, Josiah. London. Eminent Swiss maker who located in England and made one of the first lever escapements, 1780.
Etherington, George. London. 1684.
Facio, Nichlas. Born in Basle, 1664. Introduced jewelling of watches.
Fatton, Frederick Louis. London. Many fine watches in early 19th century, signed "Fatton, Paris."
Favre-Bulle, Frederic Louis. Born in Switzerland, 1770. A very fine maker.
Fister, Amon. Philadelphia. 1794.
Flant, Jehan. Geneva. Many fine watches, died 1616.
Garbier, Charles. London. Watches with this name 1705-20 may be fictitious.
Garon, Peter. London. 1694.
Gibbons, Thomas. Philadelphia. 1751.
Goddard, Luther. Shrewsbury, Mass. Early 19th century American watchmaker.
Godemar, Freres. Geneva. 1810.
Gordon, Thomas. Edinburgh. Early 18th century.
Graham. George. London. Invented dead-beat escapement and died 1715.
Gray, Benjamin. London. 1676-1764.
Gregory, Jeremie. London. Last half of 17th century.
Gretton, Charles. London. Excellent watches in early 18th century.
Guerint, Sebastien Francois. Geneva and London. 19th century.

Hackett, Simon. London. 17th century.
Harland, Thomas. Norwich, Conn. First recognized manufacturer of watches in America, from 1773 to 1806.
Henlein, Peter. Nuremburg. First known watchmaker.
Hill, Benjamin. London. 17th century.
Hillier, James. London. Watch glass maker, 1790-1810.
Hillius, Martin. Dresden. Fine watches, 1668.
Hindley, Henry. York. Watchmaker and invented the screw cutting lathe, 1740.
Holtzman, Johannis. Vienna. Watches with dial much above the movement, 1775.
Hooke, Robert. Invented the balance spring for watches. 1635-1703.
Huaud Family. Geneva. Fine enamel painters.
Hubert, Etienne. Rouen. About 1620.
Hynam, Robert. St. Petersburg. Second half of 18th century.
Ilbury, William. London. Fine enamelled watches for the Chinese market. Died 1839.
Ingold, Pierre Frederick. Paris and London. Pioneer in watchmaking machinery.
Jackman, Joseph. London. 1690.
Japy, Frederic. Pioneered machinery for watch production of factory system. 1749-1813.
Jolly, J. Paris. Worked also for Catherine de Medici, second half of 16th century.
Jones, Henry. London. Very famous 17th century maker.
Julliott, Solomon. London. 1738.
Kloch, P. Amsterdam. Enamelled watches, 1700.
Knapp, William. Annapolis. 1767.
Knibb, Joseph. Oxford. About 1690.
Knoese, J.P. Amsterdam. Excellent enamel painting on watches, about 1770.
Labe, Claude. Stuttgart. 1671-1717.
Lagis, Pierre Didier. Geneva. Died 1679.
Launay, David F. New York. 1801.
Lepine, Jean Antoine. Watchmaker to Louis XV. 1720-1814.
Leroy, Julien. Paris. Celebrated watchmaker, devised form of repeating mechanism. Died 1759.
Leroy, Pierre. Paris. His very famous son who did brilliant work on escapements.

Leukert, Johann Gottlieb. Dresden. 18th century.
Lindren, Erik. Stockholm. Born 1729.
Litherland, Peter. Liverpool. Pioneered lever watch production.
McCabe, John. Baltimore. 1774.
McGraw, Donald. Annapolis. 1767.
Markwick, James. London. 1692.
Markwick, Markham. London. To about 1805. Specialized in watches for Turkish market.
Martinot, M. Avignon. About 1700.
Massey, Edward. London. Invented the crank-roller lever escapement. 1772-1825.
Meylan, Philippe Samuel. Brassus and Geneva. Born 1770. Many unusual musical and alarm watches.
Michaud, P. Paris. About 1750.
Mudge, Thomas. London. Very famous maker, died 1794.
Murray, James. London. First half of 19th century.
Myrmecides, —. Paris. May have been the inventor of cruciform watches, about 1530.
Noakes, James. London. Died 1818.
Nordsteen, Peter. Petersburg, Stockholm, and Moscow. Latter part of 18th century.
Norton, Eardley. London. Fine maker of complicated watches from 1760.
Ortelli, A. Oxford. About 1790.
Parker, Jas. Cambridge. 1770.
Parnell, Thomas. Canterbury. 1785.
Patrick, Miles. Greenwich. 1790.
Peale, Charles Wilson. Annapolis. 1764.
Pendleton, Richard. London. From 1780.
Perigal, Francis. London. Watchmaker to the king, 1786.
Perron, L. Besancon. Fine French maker, died 1836.
Pinchbeck, Christopher. London. Fine maker of musical watches, died 1732.
Pound, Isaac. Charleston. From 1746.
Prior, Edward. London. Maker of fine watches for the Turkish market, about 1800.
Purse, Thomas. Baltimore. About 1807.
Quare, Daniel. London. Very famous maker and inventor of the repeating watch. 1648-1724.

Quelch, Richard. Oxford. About 1650.
Ramsay, David. London. Watchmaker to James I and died 1654.
Ranna, —. Vienna. About 1790.
Recordon, Louis. London. Self-winding watch. Died 1824.
Reymond, —. Charleston from Paris. 1785.
Richard, Daniel John. Introduced watchmaking to Neuchatel, Switzerland. 1672-1741.
Richter, F.J. Nuremburg. Late 17th century.
Rippon, Richard. London. Famous for repeating watches from 1810.
Rochat Frères. Geneva. About 1810.
Rodet, I. London. From 1740.
Rogers, Isaac. London. Very fine maker. 1754-1839.
Romieu, L. Rouen. About 1630.
Romilly, John. Paris. Born in Geneva 1714. Made several 8-day watches.
Rousseau, Jean. London and Geneva. Died 1684.
Sacre, Le Jeune. Paris. From 1792.
Samuel, Samuel. London. From 1772.
Sandoz, Jacques. Geneva. Travelling repeating watches, about 1750.
Savage, George. Haddersfield and London. From 1808, refined the lever escapement and invented the two-pin variety.
Schollet, John Baptist. Boston. From 1796.
Schuyler, Peter C. New York. 1802.
Seignoir, Robert. London. From about 1667.
Sermand, Jacques. Geneva. Mid-17th century
Slade, J.L. London. 1790.
Smeaton, John. York. About 1650.
Soret, Isaac. Geneva. 1673-1760.
Stanton, Edward. London. From 1655.
Street, Richard. London. From about 1687.
Syberberg, Christopher. Charleston. 1768.
Tarleton, William. Liverpool. From 1770.
Terold, Henry. Ipswich. About 1640.
Thomas, Francis. Dublin. 1750.
Tobias, Michael Isaac. Liverpool. Watch with second hand which turned four times a minute. About 1810.
Tompion, Thomas. London. One of the great English watchmakers, made some of the first watches with balance springs.
Tonckhure, Francis. Baltimore. Early 19th century.

Toulmin, Samuel. London. From 1765.
Trauner, Johann. Wurzburg. Mid-18th century.
Trott, Peter. Boston. About 1800.
Turrell, Samuel. Boston. From 1789.
Tyrer, Thomas. London. Patented the duplex escapement in 1782.
Vaart, H.G. Strassburg. About 1560.
Vallette, Ds. & Fils. Geneva. About 1785.
Vallier, Jean. Lyons. From about 1564.
Vallin, N. London. About 1600.
Van Ceulen, John. Hague. Repeating watches about 1750.
Van der Cloesen, Bernard. Hague. 1688-1719.
Vaucher, Daniel. Paris. Very fine maker, from about 1767.
Vautier, Loys. Blois. Early 17th century.
Votter, Peter. Vienna. 1764.

Vuolf, J.C. Skull watch maker, 1600.
Wagner, E.M. Berne. About 1760.
Wagstaff, Thomas. London. Until 1793.
Ward, Richard. Liverpool. From 1790.
Warner, Cuthbert. Baltimore. From 1799.
Warner, George T. New York. From 1795.
Watts, Brounker. London. From 1684.
Webster, William. London. Early 18th century.
Weckherlin, Elias. Augsburg. From mid-17th century.
Weldon, Samuel. London. 1774.
Weller, Francis. Philadelphia from London about 1777.
West, Thomas. London. From 1694.
Windmills, Joseph. London. Well known maker, from 1671.
Young, William. Bath. 1790.

Glossary

Axle. The rod on which the balance wheel revolves.

Balance cock. The projecting bar that holds one of the bearings of the balance.
Balance spring. See hairspring.
Balance staff. See axle.
Balance wheel. A wheel that regulates the movement of the watch.
Barrel. The case that holds the mainspring.
Barrel arbor. A hook on a small spool attached to the mainspring.
Basse-taille. A method of enamelling whereby a thin layer of translucent enamel is laid over an engraved plate.
Bezel. The grooved rim holding the watch crystal.

Chasing a pattern. Pounding, rubbing, or pressing from either the front or underside to create the pattern. *See* repoussé.
Champlevé. A type of enamelling whereby different colors of glass are baked into the hollowed areas of the metal dial and case.
Chronograph. A timepiece capable of extremely accurate measurement.
Cloisonné. A type of enamelling whereby the design is set into hollows outlined by strips of gold or other metal on the watch dial.

Dial train. The part that drives the hour and minute hands.

Enamelling. The process of melting colored glass onto a metal surface for decorative effect; *see also* basse-taille, champlevé, cloisonné, flinqué.
Engraving a pattern. Cutting the material away to form the pattern.
Escapement. Consisting of three parts; escape wheel, pallet, balance, to see that all wheels turn at a steady rate of speed.

Flinqué. Enamelling over a regular pattern of hand engraving.
Foliot. A horizontal crosspiece that is weighted.
Fusee. A coneshaped pulley and chain with spiral grooves used to equalize the mainspring's pull.

Hairspring. A spiral spring used to curb the motions of balance.

Jewels. Used to cut friction and increase regularity.

Mainspring. Springy, metal ribbon of different lengths, widths, and thicknesses, which unwinds and rotates the wheels.
Musk ball watch. Iron movements mounted in perforated metal spheres.

Glossary

Pavé. Jewels set so close together that no metal shows between them.
Perpetuelle. See self-winder.
Pillar. The posts, usually decorated, that hold the two plates of a watch movement together.
Pinion. A gear with a number of teeth.
Putto. A design with an often winged, cherubic infant.

Ratchet wheel. A wheel with teeth that are engaged by a pivoted bar to prevent reverse motion.
Repeater. Watch that strikes in sequence when a projecting slide is moved round or pushed in.
Repoussé. A type of chased design in bold relief made by hammering on the reverse side of the metal.

Sandglass. An hourglass.
Self-winder. A watch in which the spring winds automatically with the movements of the wearer.
Shagreen. Either sharkskin or horsehide, colored green, used as a protective case for the watch.
Stackfreed. A strong, curved spring and cam used to equalize the uneven pull of the mainspring.
Stem-winder. A keyless watch, wound by a stem in its side that turns the ratchet wheel.

Tourbillon. A revolving carriage in which the escapement was placed to avoid position errors.
Train. Consists of the mainspring and barrel drive.

Verge. A vertically mounted rod that oscillates horizontally.

Index

alarm watch, 26-27, 88
American Horologe Company,
    see Waltham Watch Company
Amidon, Captain G.H., 6
antique American watches, 55-86
Arnold, John, 25
attachments, 25-27
automatic machinery, 82-85
axle, see balance staff

back plate, 12, 16
balance, 50, 81
balance cock, 7, 21, 57
balance spring, 13, 19, 51
balance staff, 83-85
balance staff pivots, 31
balance wheel, 22, 31
Barlow, Edward, 23
barrel, 12, 32, 49, 81, 82
barrel arbor, 32, 49
barrel drive, 50
basse-taille enamelling, 18-19
Bauquer, Robert, 18
Bernard, Nichols, 18
Brandenburg, Court of, 18
Breguet, Abraham-Louis, 24-25,
    30-31, 51, 81, 88, 94, 96
Britten's, 20, 55
Buck, Daniel, 29
Buck Rogers pocket watch, 95

calendar watch, 27
cam, 12
cannon pinion, 52
catgut cord, 12
champleve enamel, 16
Chartier, Pierre, 17
chasing, 10, 20, 54
    repousse, 20, 96
chemisette, 9
Civil War, 5-6, 64, 81
clock watch, 10

cloisonné, 17
club-tooth, 62
clutch wheel, 49
collecting parts, 114
comic character watch, 95, 96
commemorative watch, 95-96
*Cosmographia Pomponii
    Melae,* 9
Cromwell, Oliver, 88
crown wheel, 10
Curtis, Samuel, 61, 62
Custer, Jacob, 57
cylinder escapement, 56

da Vinci, Leonardo, 13
death's head watch, 15
De Long, Paul, 91
Dennison, Aaron L., 58-64,
    82, 85
depreciation, 94
detent escapement, 31
dial, 7, 16, 54
dial train, 52, 53
dollar watch, 29
Donald Duck wristwatch, 95
Dubie, J., 17
duplex escapement, 29, 82

electronic quartz watch, 30
Elizabeth I, 5, 25
Emery, Josiah, 29
enamelling, 16-19, 113
    basse-taille, 18-19
    champlevé, 16
    cloisonné, 17
    flinqué, 19
    hard enamel, 16
    soft enamel, 16
engraving, 10, 54
equation-of-time watch, 27
escapement, 7, 29-30, 31, 49,
    50, 53, 56, 57, 82, 88

Index

cylinder, 56
detent, 31
duplex, 29, 82
forked, *see* lever watch
lever, 31, 57, 88
pin-pallet, 29-30
verge, 49
escape pivot, 81
escape wheel, 50

Facio, Nichlas, 54
fakes, 114-116
fixed central arbor, 12
flinque, 19
Floucher, Blase, 17
Flurnoy, Benjamin, 92, 93
foliot balance, 10
forked escapement, *see* lever watch
fritillary, 16
fusee, 7, 12-14, 15, 29, 49

Garland, Matilda, 91
Garland, Reverend Rufus, 91, 92, 93
Goddard, Luther, 56-57
goldsmith, 11
gold watch, 113-114
gongs, 23
Gribelin, Isaac, 17

hairspring, *see* balance spring
hallmark, 7, 28
hard enamel, 16
Harland, Thomas, 56
Harper, W.E., 57
Hautefeuille, Abbe de, 19, 51
Heinlein, Peter, *see* Henlein, Peter
Hele, Peter, *see* Henlein, Peter
Henle, Peter, *see* Henlein, Peter
Henlein, Peter, 9, 32
hog's bristle, 19, 51
Hooke, Robert, 19, 51
horsehide, 20
hour wheel, 52

Howard, Edward, 58-64, 82, 85
Huaud, Jean and Ami, 18
Huaud, Pierre, 18
Hughenin, Gustavus, 24
Huon, Jacques, 17
Huygens, Christian, 19, 51

indicating mechanism, 52
Ingersoll, R.H., 82, 95
isochronism, 81

Jacquard, Antoine, 15
James II, 23
Japy, Frederic, 86
jewels, 54, 81

karussel, 31
keyless watch, 24-25

lady's watch, 64
Lafayette, Marquis de, 5, 88-93
lapidary casemaker, 11
lever escapement, 31, 57, 88
lever watch, 28-29
Litherland, Peter, 29
L. Leroy & Cie., 28
Lone Ranger wristwatch, 95

machine-made watch, 29
mainspring, 9, 10, 12, 29, 32, 50, 61
Margetts, George, 28
Mary, Queen of Scots, 87
mass production, 58, 60-62
Metropolitan Museum of Art, 27
Midnall, John, 88
miniature watches, 25
minute hand, 53-54
minute wheel, 52
Mix, Tom, 5, 95
Morliere, Christophe, 17
Mudge, Thomas, 29
musical watch, 28
musk ball, 10

Nuremberg eggs, 10

overcoil, 51
overcoil hairspring, 31

painting in enamel, 17
pair cases, 19-20
pair case watch, 27-28
pallet, 50, 81
pattern book, 15
parachute, 31
Pearson, E.A., 25
pedometer watch, 24
pendulum watch, 21-22
perpetuelle, 24-25, 88
Philippe, Adrien, 24
pillar, 7, 12, 20-21, 82
pinion, 12, 32, 50, 84
pin-pallet escapement, 29-30
Pitkin, Henry, 57-58, 82, 85
Pitkin, James, 57-58
pocket watch, 15, 19, 30, 31
Poetl, Jacques, 17
pornographic watch, 31
potash, 16
Premier Maximus Certificate Watch, 81
Prussia, Court of, 18
Puritan watch, 21

Quare, Daniel, 23

rack striking works, 23
railroad watch, 30, 94
ratchet-tooth, 62
ratchet wheel, 49
repeater watch, 23, 25, 26, 28, 56
repousse chasing, 20, 96
ring watch, 25
Robbins, Royal E., 64
rocking bar mechanism, 24
Roscopf watch, 29-30
Royal Scottish Museum, 87
ruby cylinder, 31

sandglass, 13, 14
Sargeant, Jacob, 57, 58
setting mechanism, 52-53
shagreen, 19-20, 88, 89
sharkskin, 20
shifting sleeve, 24
skull watch, 87
Smithsonian Institution, 93
soft enamel, 16
Souvenirs of Duguay-Trouin, 13
split bezel ring, 16
stackfreed, 12-14, 15, 49
striking watch, 26, 87
Swiss watch, 85-86

tact watch, 31
Thomson, Richard, 24
tourbillon, 29, 31, 82
Toutin, Jean, 17
Tracy, Baker & Co., 64
train, 50
tulip pillar, 20

unusual watches, 27-28

Vauquer, Michel, 18
verge, 10, 56, 57
verge escapement, 49
Victoria and Albert Museum, 17
Victoria, Queen, 88

Waltham Watch Company, 61
Ward, John R., 88-89, 90
Washington, George, 89
watchcock, 114
watch glasses, 16
watch key, 23
Waterbury Long Wind, 82
winding crown, 49
winding mechanism, 49, 53
winding pinion, 49
winding square, 12
winding wheel, 49
wrist watch, 25, 30

Zech, Jacob, 12